DON'T PANIC!
You *can* fix your PC

WE ALL KNOW what computers are like: they're just about tuned to your liking, you're in the middle of something really important and, bang, they break. If this sounds familiar to you, don't worry, as this book will help you fix your PC if it goes wrong.

Each chapter deals with a specific type of problem and begins with a flowchart that will help you track down the problem areas. Once you've worked out what has made your computer stop working, our in-depth, jargon-free step-by-step guides will help you fix it.

Even if you don't have a problem with your computer at the moment you should buy this book, as prevention really is better than a cure. With step-by-step workshops on how to back up, restore and tune your PC, you'll find that you can avoid the majority of problems and recover quicker from anything that does go wrong.

As overheating hardware can cause lots of trouble, we'll even show you how to give your PC a spring clean, so you can be sure that it will keep working smoothly.

We're confident that this guide will help you fix the vast majority of problems with your computer, but there are times when you'll either need to call for help or buy replacement kit. Even here, you'll find this book incredibly useful. By helping you track down the problem, you'll need to spend less time on a support call as you'll be able to explain exactly what's gone wrong. You'll then get the support you need and an answer to your problem even quicker.

So, whether you've got a problem now or are worried about suffering one later, don't panic: this book will get your computer working again.

David Ludlow, Editor
david_ludlow@dennis.co.uk

Contents

The Complete PC Repair Manual

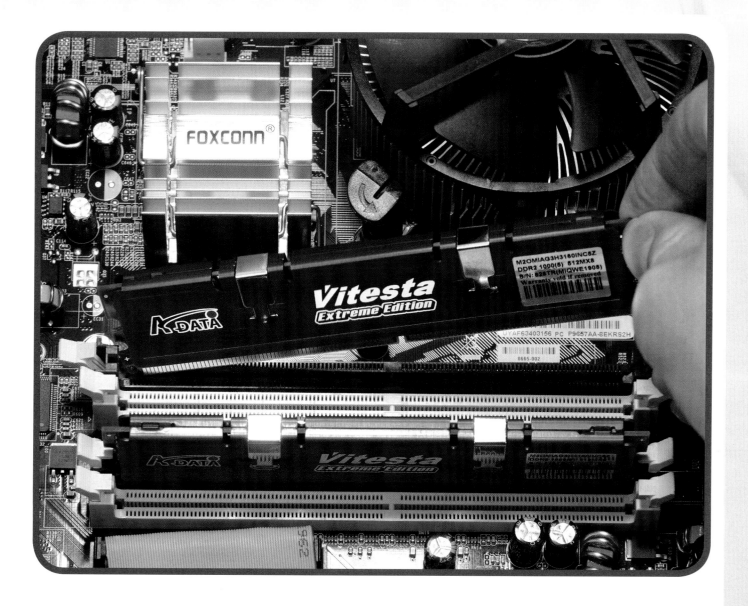

Into the BIOS 102

The BIOS controls all the hardware in your PC and can be responsible for a range of faults. Here we show you how to configure the BIOS properly and where to go when you need to troubleshoot

Operating systems 110

Sometimes a fault's so bad that you have to reinstall Windows. Our step-by-step instructions will help you with Windows Vista and XP

Testing 120

Once you think you've found the cause of a problem, testing your components can help confirm your diagnosis. Here we show you how to do it

Glossary 142

Baffled by some computer jargon or confused about what a certain connector does? Find out what it all means in our jargon-busting guide

Chapter 1

Essentials

MOST PC PROBLEMS are easier to fix than you think, and can usually be solved by following a few simple steps.
In this chapter we'll show you all the common fixes to try first for both hardware and Windows problems. We'll also run through the essential skills that anyone looking to repair their PC should know about.

Top 10 TIPS

IF YOUR COMPUTER has just broken down, the good news is that it's probably not that difficult to fix. Start by following our top 10 tips and you're likely to get it working again quickly.

① MAKE ONE CHANGE AT A TIME

Before you start working on your computer, you should remember to try only one fix at a time before seeing if your computer is working. Doing it this way means you'll be able to track down exactly what caused the problem. This is incredibly useful, as you'll know exactly what to do if you ever get the same problem again.

Making lots of changes in one go may work, but you'll be left guessing as to exactly what you did to fix your PC. Get the same problem again and you'll be just as much in the dark as the first time you suffered from it.

② TURN IT OFF AND BACK ON AGAIN

This may sound like the sarcastic response that all customer helplines give, but there's a good reason it's used so often: it really works. Computers are strange beasts at the best of times, and restarting them sorts out all manner of things. For the best results, you should take the power cable out, after shutting Windows down properly, and count to 10.

You should do the same with other devices, such as wireless routers, that have a problem.

③ CHECK CABLES

It may sound obvious, but we've lost count of the number of PCs that we thought were broken, but actually just had cables that had become detached. Before you get the screwdriver out, make sure that everything's still plugged into your computer. Check your other devices as well: cables are just as likely to drop out of your monitor and printer as they are to come out of your PC. Check that the power supply is turned on at the switch on its rear, too. You should also check that the internal cables haven't become loose.

For USB devices, it often helps to unplug them and reconnect them to a different USB port. This forces your computer and Windows to redetect them.

For more information on how to check internal and external cables, see page 123.

④ UNDO WHAT YOU JUST DID

A large proportion of computer troubles are caused when new hardware or software is installed. If you've recently run into a problem, think about what you've just done and then reverse the action. So, for example, if you've just installed a new application, remove it (see page 13 for more advice); new hardware should be removed from the computer.

Problems can also be caused by Windows downloading updates. You can either remove them one by one using Windows' program manager (see page 13) or by performing a System Restore (see page 12), which will return your computer's state to an earlier date.

⑤ USE SAFE MODE

If you can't start Windows to uninstall software or run System Restore, use Windows' Safe Mode option. Turn on your PC and press F8

---

① **Turning your computer off and back on again can fix a surprisingly large number of problems**

② **Starting your PC in Safe Mode can help you remove damaged hardware and software**

③ **If the Num Lock or Caps Lock lights can be toggled, your computer hasn't crashed**

④ **Event Viewer can tell you what's wrong with your computer**

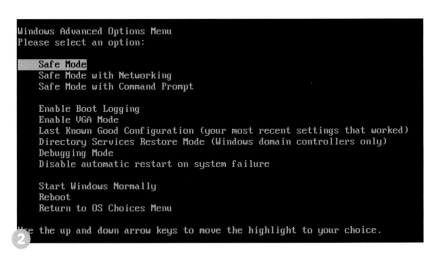

```
Windows Advanced Options Menu
Please select an option:

    Safe Mode
    Safe Mode with Networking
    Safe Mode with Command Prompt

    Enable Boot Logging
    Enable VGA Mode
    Last Known Good Configuration (your most recent settings that worked)
    Directory Services Restore Mode (Windows domain controllers only)
    Debugging Mode
    Disable automatic restart on system failure

    Start Windows Normally
    Reboot
    Return to OS Choices Menu

Use the up and down arrow keys to move the highlight to your choice.
```

until you get the Advanced Options Menu. Select Safe Mode from the list and press Enter. You'll get a cut-down version of Windows that doesn't load all the drivers and software, but it should be enough to remove damaged applications and hardware and run System Restore.

6 RESEAT HARDWARE

Over time the components in your computer can become dislodged or clogged up with dust. Simply taking your PC apart, reseating all the hardware and cleaning the inside with an air duster can work wonders. Follow the instructions on how to clean your PC (see page 90) and reseat your hardware (pages 136-141).

7 CHECK NUM LOCK

This is a bit of an odd one, but it works. When you press Caps Lock or Num Lock on your keyboard, indicator lights turn on and off. If you have a problem with your computer, the lights no longer respond to the keys. So, if you suspect your computer has crashed, try pressing Num Lock. If it doesn't work, your PC has locked up: what software where you running? This is likely to be the cause, but check the Windows Event Viewer logs for more information (see page 42).

If you don't see anything onscreen when you turn your computer on, try pressing Num Lock. If the light doesn't work, you've got a serious hardware fault; if the light works, your PC is technically working and hasn't locked up, but there's a less serious fault.

8 LISTEN FOR TROUBLE

Computer problems often manifest themselves audibly, so listen out for trouble. If you turn your computer on and hear lots of beeps, your computer's BIOS – the part of your PC that checks hardware before Windows starts – is telling you what's wrong. These beeps aren't random noises, but structured codes that can help you track down where the problem lies.

These beep codes differ from manufacturer to manufacturer, but our guide (page 32) will help you understand what your computer is saying to you.

9 UPDATE YOUR DRIVERS

As your computer gets older, you may find that hardware stops working correctly. The main reason for this is that your drivers have become out

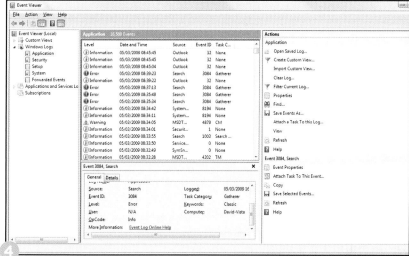

of date. The easiest way to fix the problems is to download driver updates for your hardware. For most people, updating the graphics card, motherboard and sound card drivers is enough to fix most problems (see page 10).

10 LOOK OUT FOR MESSAGES

Hardware and software manufacturers all recognise that at some point there's likely to be a problem and do their best to display error messages to help you. Look out for these, as they'll tell you what's wrong. Where possible, note down a message in full, together with any error codes you see. You can use the messages and codes to search online for a solution to your problem, and you'll most likely find a way to fix it.

As a problem can sometimes cause Windows to crash, you should check the Event Viewer (see page 42) to find out what went wrong.

Essential skills

BEFORE YOU OPEN your PC and start pulling bits out in the hope that you'll be able to fix it, there are some safety lessons to learn. You should also learn these key skills in order to make repairing your computer easier. Without these, you run the risk of damaging your computer even more, creating extra problems. The worst part is that most of the time, you'll be unable to tell that you've caused any extra damage until you try and turn your PC back on. At this point, tracking the problem down can be a real nightmare.

Here we'll take you through the main pitfalls you'll face when fixing your computer and, more importantly, how to avoid them.

STATIC ELECTRICITY

We all know about static electricity: it's the charge that builds up when we walk across a carpet and discharges when we touch someone else. This little flash of electricity may not seem very powerful, but it's potentially fatal for sensitive electronic components. Get a build-up of static and touch your processor, and you may have destroyed one of the most expensive parts of your computer.

Fortunately, avoiding problems isn't that hard. Wear an anti-static wrist strap if you've got one. This will prevent static electricity from building up, making it safe to touch any component in your computer. If you haven't got one, don't panic, as there are other ways around the problem. Try and work near a radiator. To discharge any build-up of static, simply touch the unpainted part of a radiator. You should do this at regular intervals, and certainly each time before touching a component. You're then safe to work.

Finally, all computer components come in anti-static bags. If you have any of these left over from your computer, get them out: you can rest components safely on these while you work.

MAGNETIC SCREWDRIVER

Inside your PC, you'll find that there are lots of parts of your case that are awkward to reach to screw or unscrew components. The easiest way to deal with this problem is to use a magnetic screwdriver. Simply place the screw into the screwdriver and then manoeuvre the screw towards its position. The opposite is true when removing screws, as a gentle action should mean that a screw comes away attached to the screwdriver, rather than dropping to the floor.

Don't worry about magnetically sensitive devices inside your PC. A magnetic screwdriver isn't powerful enough to cause any damage or wipe any data.

THE RIGHT SCREWS

While the right screwdriver can make your job easier, it's essential to use the right screws to prevent damage. If you're replacing or removing a device, make sure that you know which screws go where. Put a screw that's too long into a hard disk, for example, and you could damage a circuit board and break the whole thing.

If you do get your screws mixed up, it shouldn't be too hard to work out which ones to use. Of the different types of screws that are used, the small, stubby ones are for hard disks and optical drives, the long screws are for holding expansion cards in place, while the screws with the flat heads are for fitting the motherboard and for some case panels. Make sure that you don't overtighten screws, or you could cause damage. The idea is to tighten

① **Prevent the build-up of static by wearing an anti-static wrist strap**

② **Choose the right screw for the right job**

③ **Make sure that the cables are all plugged in properly**

④ **A magnetic screwdriver is an essential tool**

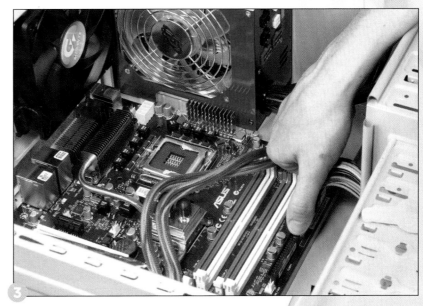

screws to the point where your components are held snugly in place, but no further.

USE THE RIGHT AMOUNT OF FORCE

When you plug components such as expansion cards, memory and a processor into your motherboard, it can be difficult to know how much force you should apply. Our tips should help you get it right. First, make sure that you've lined up your components correctly with the slot or socket – our step-by-step guides on reseating hardware (see pages 136-141) will show you how to do this.

Next, make sure that you're applying equal pressure across the device to move it into position. Processors should drop into place with little pressure, memory needs a firm push to click it into place, while expansion cards need a fair push. If you meet a lot of resistance, check that the card or memory stick is lined up properly and start again.

POWER CABLES

When repairing a PC, it's important to remember you're dealing with an electrical device. Before you plug the power in and turn on your computer, check that you've plugged all the power cables in properly, particularly on the motherboard. Loose connections can cause problems.

The fans inside a PC can cause problems, too, particularly if there are power cables near them. Make sure that all power-carrying cables are clipped out of the way of fans so that you don't cut

through them. Power connectors plug in only one way, so if you can't get one in make sure that it's the right way round. Forcing a connector in the wrong way will damage your devices irreparably.

Before you plug in your power cable, make sure that your power supply is set to the correct voltage. Some supplies have a switch that changes the voltage from 110V (US) to 230V (UK). If you've set it to 110V, the supply will be damaged and your motherboard may be affected, too.

TAKE YOUR TIME

The best tip we can give is to follow each step carefully and take your time. Repairing a PC isn't a race and, as you're dealing with lots of expensive components, it's best to get it right the first time around. Our step-by-step help will guide you through every step you need to take.

Finding and installing drivers

1 ATI gives you a choice of files to download, but the full Catalyst Control Suite is the best choice for new computers

2 You'll need to perform several file downloads in order to get the latest motherboard drivers

3 You can find the latest drivers for all your devices on the internet

4 Nvidia has a unified driver architecture, so a single download is all you need

ANY HARDWARE INSTALLED in your computer has a driver that tells Windows how it works and how it should be used. Over time these drivers can become out of date, and new applications may not work correctly. Some drivers, such as those for graphics cards, can even make your computer work faster. It's worth downloading and updating your drivers on a regular basis.

A second reason to download drivers is if you're reinstalling Windows. Having the latest drivers from the internet is better than using the ones provided on the disc, as they'll be up to date. If you can't download drivers before installing Windows, simply use the drivers that came on the disc until you've got a working computer, and then follow these instructions to download the latest drivers and install them afterwards. Thanks to the internet, getting drivers is incredibly easy and shouldn't take too long.

MOTHERBOARDS

The motherboard is the main part of your PC and it comes with plenty of built-in features, including onboard sound, networking, storage drivers and potentially even graphics. Windows, particularly Vista, will have drivers for many of these things, but if you want the best performance and the best range of features, you'll need the latest drivers.

You can get everything for your motherboard from the manufacturer's website. You'll find the address in your motherboard's manual. If not, then use a search engine to find the URL.

Once you're on the website, there should be a link for Support. Just keep following the links for motherboards and drivers. Eventually, you'll get to a point where you'll need to enter the details of your motherboard to locate the driver download page for your model. It's vital you get exactly the right model in order to get the correct drivers for your computer. If you can't find the details on the box or in the manual, then the motherboard's name is usually written on the board itself.

After you've entered your motherboard's details, you'll be presented with a long list of drivers divided by type, such as graphics or networking. For each heading, download one driver, making sure that you select the latest version. Most driver packages cater for all versions of Windows, but check the details to ensure that you download the correct driver for your operating system.

GRAPHICS CARDS

If you're using onboard graphics, you'll be able to find the latest drivers on the motherboard manufacturer's website. If you're using a dedicated graphics card, you should download the drivers directly from ATI's or Nvidia's sites. This will ensure that you get the best performance and stability from your graphics card.

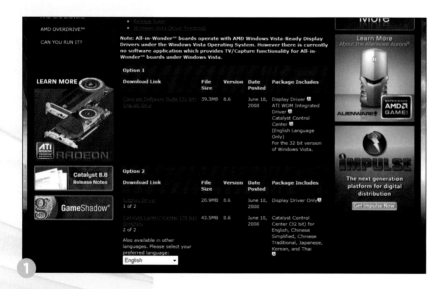

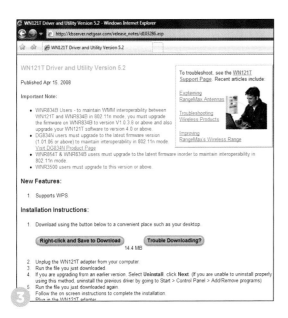

NVIDIA

Nvidia uses a unified driver package, so one download will work for most of its graphics cards. This makes installation simple. Visit *www.nvidia. com* and select Download Drivers from the Download Drivers menu in the top-left of the screen. Select the type of card (GeForce for consumer graphics cards) and the series of card that you have, such as 9xxx series for a GeForce 9600 GT. Select your language as English (UK) and click Search. Tick the box to accept the licence agreement and click Download.

It's important to select your graphics card model, as not every driver package has the driver for every graphics card. If you download the wrong package, your card won't be detected and the driver will be unable to be updated.

ATI

ATI has a similar unified driver architecture to Nvidia. Visit *http://ati.amd.com/gb-uk* and click on Support & Drivers. Click on the Download graphics drivers link. On the next page, select which operating system you'll be using, select Radeon from the list (consumer graphics cards are all Radeon models), and then select your card. Click Go to be taken to the driver selection page.

You should select Catalyst Software Suite, as this includes the driver and the Catalyst Control Panel for configuring settings. Make sure you select your model of graphics card from the list, or you may get a version of the driver that doesn't support your card.

OTHER DEVICES

If you're installing other hardware, such as a wireless network adaptor, TV tuner, sound card or printer, you'll need to download the latest drivers for these, too. In a similar way to the procedure we've described above, you'll need to visit the manufacturer's website and follow the links until you get to where you can select which device you want to download drivers for. Check a device's manual for full details on the manufacturer's website. If you can't find any information, a Google search for the manufacturer's name should bring up the details you need. Remember to make sure that you get the right driver for your device and for the operating system that you require.

REGULAR CHECKS

Once you've got the latest drivers, your job isn't done. You should regularly check manufacturers' websites and see if updates are available. Typically, graphics card drivers are updated monthly, while other devices are updated less regularly.

Driver updates fix known problems and can help your PC become more stable and perform better, while some even add new features. It's worth going back to a manufacturer's site regularly to check for updates if you're suffering from a problem, as a new driver can often fix this.

Manufacturers' websites are also useful if you want help with a product. You can also find manuals for download, which can be really helpful if you lose your printed version and need to check a detail or plan an upgrade.

TIP
New versions of drivers can sometimes fix problems with your computer. If you're having trouble with a particular device, look for a newer driver before doing anything else.

HOW TO...
Restore your system

IF YOU'RE HAVING problems, System Restore – which is built into Windows XP and Vista – allows you to return your PC to a working state.

1 TURN IT ON

First, make sure System Restore is on. Press the Windows+Break keys. Click the System Restore tab at the top (in Vista, click the System protection button), and make sure the box marked Turn off System Restore isn't ticked (in Vista, make sure that drive C is ticked). There must be at least 200MB of free space on your hard disk for System Restore to work. If there isn't, you'll need to clear out unwanted files.

In XP, use the slider to specify how much disk space System Restore is allowed to use; the more it has, the more restore points it can keep. Vista has automatic settings.

2 CREATE A RESTORE POINT

Every time you make a significant change to your system, such as installing a new application, Windows automatically creates a restore point. It's good practice to create a restore point manually before you make any changes, though, so you know that you have something to fall back on.

To create a restore point, go to Start, All Programs, Accessories, System Tools, System Restore. Choose Create a restore point, and follow the wizard. In Vista, click Open System Protection and click the Create button.

3 RESTORE YOUR SYSTEM

When your PC has a problem, you can revert to any saved restore point. If you know which software is causing the problem, remove it using Add/ Remove Programs. If it's a driver, turn off your PC and remove the relevant hardware, too. Next, with your PC running, open System Restore as before and this time choose Restore my computer to an earlier time. Click Next and choose a restore point (Vista chooses one automatically, but you can click Choose a different restore point instead). Pay close attention to the date: use the latest point when you're sure the system worked properly. Allow the restore to finish and your PC to restart.

4 EMERGENCY RESTORE

If something has gone really wrong, your PC may not even boot into Windows. While the PC is booting, keep pressing F8. Instead of the normal Windows startup routine, you'll be offered a menu. Choose Safe Mode with command prompt. Log on as an administrator, and at the command prompt type c:\windows\system32\restore\rstrui.exe (in Vista, type c:\windows\system32\rstrui.exe). This starts System Restore, and you can then choose a restore point to go back to.

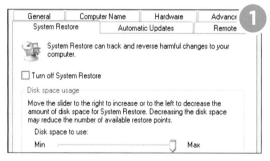

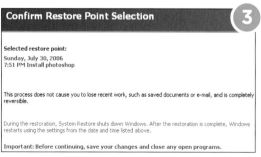

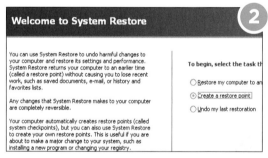

HOW TO...
Uninstall software

A TROUBLESOME PIECE of software can cause problems, and should be removed. If a problem has just occurred, then it could well be an update that Windows has just downloaded. Again, these should be removed. If you can't start your computer, reboot it, tap F8 and select Safe Mode. This will let you start your computer in a diagnostic mode. Here, we'll show you how to remove unwanted programs and Windows updates.

① START THE PROGRAM MANAGER
All the programs on your computer are managed using Windows' application manager. To start it in Vista, go to the Control Panel and click Uninstall a program (listed under Programs). In XP, select Add/Remove Programs in the Control Panel.

② REMOVE AN APPLICATION IN VISTA
Windows Vista and XP have a similar view of the applications that are installed, but the steps to remove an application differ slightly. In Vista, select the program you want to remove. If there's an Uninstall button at the top, click this and follow the onscreen instructions. Otherwise, click the Change button and follow the onscreen instructions until you see an option to uninstall. The Change option will usually let you add and remove different components, such as removing one application from a suite. If there's a Repair button, you can try this, which will reinstall the application from scratch using the manufacturer's settings.

③ REMOVE AN APPLICATION IN XP
In XP, click the application you want to uninstall and click Remove or Change/Remote. Follow the onscreen instructions to remove the program. Some applications will give you a Repair option, which you can use to reinstall the software.

④ REMOVE WINDOWS UPDATES
Windows updates can sometimes cause problems, and you may need to remove the latest ones if you've run into problems. In Vista, click View installed updates. You can change the sorting of the list by clicking on the column headers. For example, selecting Installed On will sort updates by the install date. Select the update you want to remove and click Uninstall. In Windows XP, select Show updates, select the update you want to uninstall and click the Remove button. ⬯

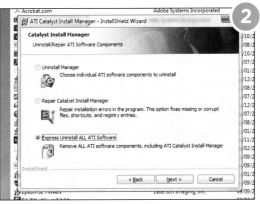

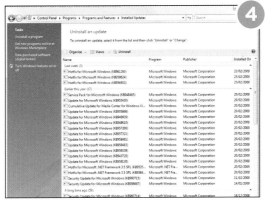

💡 TIP
If you can't uninstall a program, try installing it again and then removing it.

HOW TO...
Recover deleted files

THE SAFEST WAY to make sure that you don't lose any files is to make a backup of your computer (see page 84). However, deleting a file before you've run a backup isn't fatal.

When you delete a file from your hard disk, its space is merely marked as being available, giving you a chance to recover it. We'll show you how to do this with the free PC Inspector File Recovery (*http://tinyurl.com/pcinspector*) application.

Install this software before you need it. If you haven't had a chance to do this, download and install the application on a different drive from which you want to recover the files, if possible. This will stop File Recovery from overwriting the disk space that your deleted files are occupying.

1 SCAN YOUR DRIVES
When you start the application, you should select which language you want to use and then click the green tick icon. On the next screen, click any of the icons on the left-hand side of the screen. File Recovery will then search your computer for hard disks from which it can recover files.

2 CHOOSE DRIVE TO RECOVER FILES FROM
Depending on your computer, you may see twice as many choices as there are drives. Ignore the top set that have 'Windows drive' written next to them,

as these are duplicates of the bottom set. Find the drive, such as C:, with your missing files on it and click it. Click the green tick icon.

3 SCAN FOR LOST FILES
After scanning your hard disk for existing files and folders, you'll be prompted to scan for lost files (those that have been deleted through an error or hard disk corruption). Ignore the sliders and options and simply click the green tick icon. Your entire hard disk will be searched, which could take anything up to a couple of hours.

4 SELECT FILES TO RECOVER
Once the scan has completed, you can choose the files to recover. Click on Deleted to find files that you've deleted. Right-click on any file or folder and click Save to. You'll be prompted to choose a location to save the files. To be on the safe side, pick a different hard disk or you run the risk of overwriting other deleted files.

You can do the same thing with the Lost folder, although files may have lost their original names and be called things such as cluster0001.jpg. Save any files of the type that match your missing files, and sort through them later. Finally, click the third icon on the left (a magnifying glass) and you can filter the results by searching; for example, *.jpg will find all JPEG picture files.

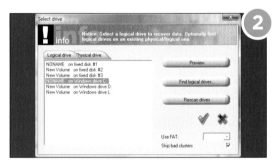
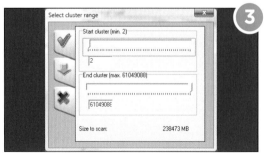

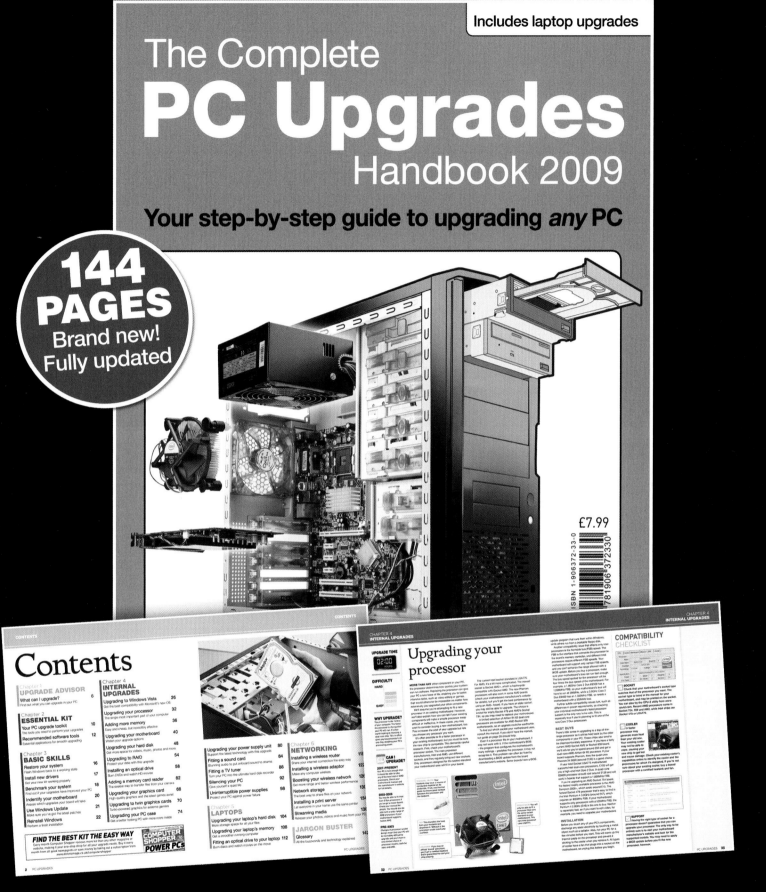

Troubleshooting Windows

1 Device Manager shows you if any of your hardware isn't installed properly

2 Windows' System Information screen tells you what hardware has been detected

3 Software manufacturers routinely release patches for their software, which can fix bugs and introduce compatibility for newer operating systems

ALTHOUGH WINDOWS HAS improved a lot since its early days, there are still times when it will give you a headache and simply refuse to work properly. This can be frustrating, particularly if it's been working without any trouble until now. Fortunately, the problems aren't usually fatal and can be solved with a bit of perseverance.

Over the next few pages, we'll talk you through some common problem-solving techniques to help you get your PC back on track. The most important thing you can do is be methodical and rule out one problem at a time. If you do too much in one go, you might solve the problem, but you'll never know its source, which could cause trouble further down the line.

In most cases, problems with getting peripherals or other hardware to work are usually caused by the drivers you've installed. Most of the time, simply using the Add/Remove Programs option in the Control Panel to delete the offending driver or software and installing a new one will fix your woes (see page 13 for details). In other cases, downloading the latest drivers from the device manufacturer's website will fix the problem.

UNSTABLE WINDOWS CRASHES

If you find that your computer keeps crashing and you've made sure that your hardware isn't getting too hot (see page 132), then the problem is probably down to one of two things: hardware compatibility or software compatibility.

In either case, note down any error messages that appear. If you type the exact phrase into a search engine, there's a good chance you'll find a website that will tell you what caused the problem and how to fix it. Look for tell-tale signs in the error message, as Windows will usually say which bit of software or hardware has caused the problem. You can then look for support from the relevant manufacturer.

If your computer just crashes or the error message isn't particularly helpful, remember what you were doing when your computer crashed. If it always occurs when you open a particular application, then it's probably that piece of software causing the problem. This is especially likely to be the case if you're installing an old application that you used in an earlier version of Windows.

Fortunately, most manufacturers carry updates for software on their website, so visit the relevant site and look for a new update (see page 10). If you've just updated your version of Windows, you may need to upgrade to a newer version of the application that is compatible with your version of Windows. Look for upgrade offers, as these usually provide you with the latest version of the software at a reduced price.

HARDWARE

If your PC crashes randomly and not always when you're using a particular bit of software, then it's probably a piece of hardware that's misbehaving or hasn't been properly detected. Don't worry, as this is easy to check.

First, right-click Computer in the Start menu (My Computer in Windows XP) and select Properties. This will display System Information windows that will tell you which processor is installed and how much memory your PC has. If this information doesn't match up with what you expect to see, then you've probably got a problem. You should try and reseat the memory and processor, and read the section on setting up your BIOS (see page 102) to find out how to get your computer to detect your hardware properly.

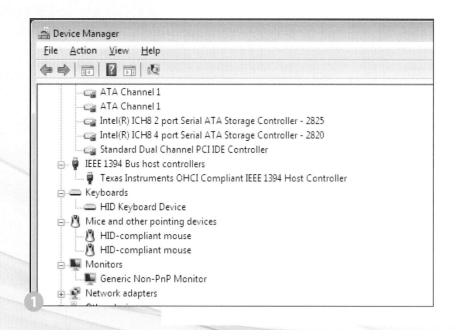

If everything is detected properly here, then it could be another bit of hardware that's causing the problem. To see if this is the case, you need to check Device Manager. In Vista, right-click on Computer and select Properties. Click on the Device Manager link on the right-hand side. In XP, right-click on My Computer, select Properties, click on the hardware tab and select Device Manager.

If any devices aren't installed properly, a yellow warning triangle containing an exclamation mark will be displayed. This is Windows' way of highlighting a problem. If the warning icon is next to an Unknown Device, then the problem is probably that you haven't installed all the necessary drivers. Go back through your list of downloaded drivers (see page 10) and make sure that you installed everything. If you did, then you should check your device manufacturers' websites to make sure that you downloaded everything you were supposed to. The motherboard manufacturer's site is worth checking, as it's easy to miss a driver download.

If the warning triangle is next to a known device, then its driver is not working properly. First, try and reinstall the driver. If that doesn't work, you may have an incompatible driver and should check the manufacturer's website for an updated version. You should also look for compatibility information online to make sure that the device is compatible with your operating system. Our guide to using Device Manager (see page 38) will give you more advice on how to use this tool to troubleshoot and fix hardware problems.

SPECIFIC HARDWARE NOT WORKING

The steps above give you information on hardware problems where an error has been detected, but just because a device is listed correctly in Device Manager, this doesn't mean it's working properly. Here we'll examine some of the most common pieces of hardware and take you through some troubleshooting techniques.

KEYBOARDS AND MICE

Windows has built-in drivers, so any keyboard or mouse that you plug in should work automatically. However, while you'll get all the basic functions if

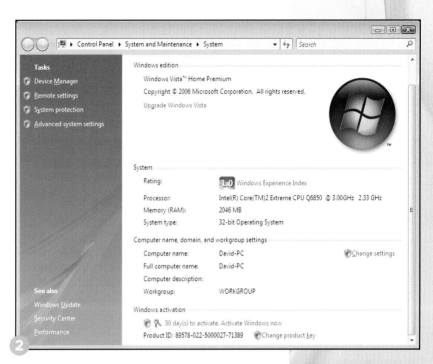

you have a keyboard with extra controls, such as buttons to control volume and media playback, or a mouse with programmable buttons, you'll still need to install the manufacturer's software.

This will be easy to find by visiting the manufacturer's website and searching the support section for your product. Once you have downloaded and installed the recommended software, you should find that all your buttons will

TIP
Check the manufacturer's support forums for help on a specific problem. Chances are that if you're having a problem, someone else will have already encountered it and has a solution.

start working correctly. You should also use the Regional Settings Control Panel options to check that your computer is set to the correct region.

AUDIO

If you're using a dedicated sound card, you should read its manual for full instructions on how to install it, as well as troubleshooting advice. Windows will automatically install sound drivers for your onboard sound, but they're not as good as the real drivers. If you're having problems, make sure that you've installed the proper ones from your manufacturer.

If you can't get the sound working at all, there are several things you can check. With most onboard sound, you should notice an icon in the Notification Area (to the left of the time), which looks like a speaker. Double-click this to bring up the audio management software. Your speaker configuration should be set to match the number of speakers that you have. It's worth checking at this point that your speakers or headphones are connected to the right ports on your motherboard. Check your board's manual for full details.

You can also test your sound inside Windows' Control Panel. In Vista, open the Control Panel from the Start menu and select Hardware and Sound, Manage Audio Devices. Right-click the audio device you want to use and select Test. This will play a sound through each of your speakers. If you only hear it through some of the speakers, you either have a faulty connection somewhere – in which case you should plug all the cables in again

– or you haven't told Windows the correct speaker setup you're using.

Finally, the sound output you're using should have a tick next to it. If it doesn't, it's not the default device. Right-click it and select Set as default device. Click on OK to apply the settings.

In XP, select Sounds, Speech and Audio Devices, Sounds and Audio Devices from the Control Panel. Click Advanced under Speaker settings to choose your speaker setup. Click on Audio to choose your default playback device. There's no way to test your speakers, as with Vista, so play an MP3 file to test your audio output.

GRAPHICS CARDS

In order for you to be able to see the desktop before you've had a chance to install the proper graphics card drivers, Windows can use a generic display driver that works with all cards. So just because you can see something onscreen, it doesn't mean your graphics card is set up properly.

In Device Manager, expand the Display adaptors section and see what's listed. If the full name of your graphics card isn't there and it says something like Generic VGA adaptor, your drivers aren't installed properly. For onboard graphics cards, download the drivers from the motherboard manufacturer's website.

For graphics cards, make sure you have the latest driver from Nvidia's or ATI's website. With either company, it's important to fill out the request forms properly, as doing so will take you to the latest driver for your card. Not all downloads

1 Your sound card should have a control panel where you can test your PC's audio

2 Windows can help you choose which audio device you want to use for sound

3 Vista's Network and Sharing Center is used to manage all your network settings

4 To use the new graphical features of Windows Vista, you need to enable Aero

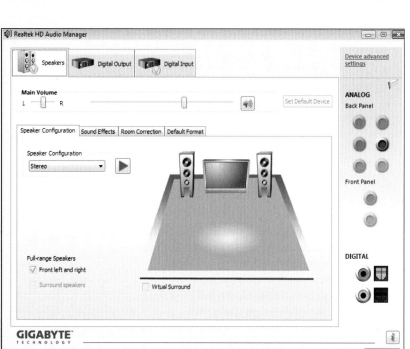

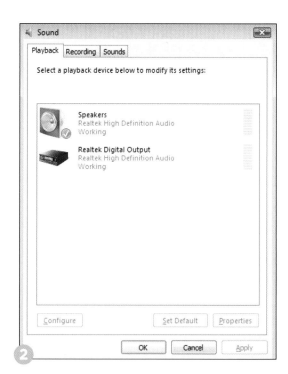

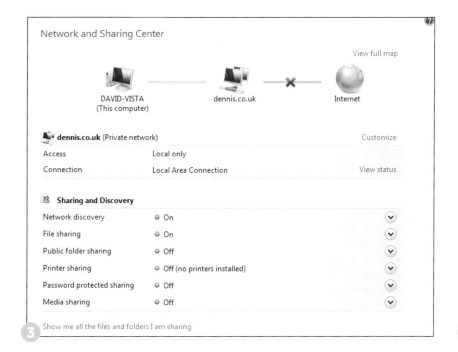

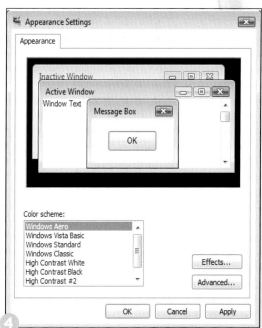

contain information for all cards, though. The latest Nvidia driver, for example, may not have drivers for a GeForce 8800 GTS graphics card, so trying to install from that will display an error message.

Once your graphics card is correctly installed, you can check that it's working by pressing Windows-R, typing dxdiag and pressing Enter. This will show you details of your hardware and tell you which version of DirectX (which is required for playing games) you're running. Those of you running Vista will be using DirectX 10, while XP owners should be running DirectX 9.0c. If dxdiag doesn't work in XP or you're running an older version of it, update to version 9.0c on Microsoft's website (*http://tinyurl.com/directxinstall*).

If you're running Vista and find that you can't use some of the new features, such as Flip3D (this turns all open windows into a 3D slideshow, and is accessed by pressing the Windows key), then it's because Aero has been turned off. Aero is the new Windows manager, and is only turned on when a graphics card that supports its features is detected. All too often, though, Windows can't properly detect a dedicated graphics card at installation, and so turns this feature off.

To turn it back on, right-click on the desktop and select Personalize. Select Windows Color and Appearance, choose Windows Aero from the list and click OK.

WIRELESS NETWORK ADAPTORS

If you're using wireless networking and have installed your network adaptor, you may find that Windows' wireless network configuration tool can't see any networks. In all likelihood, this is because your wireless adaptor has installed its own management software. You can use this application to control access to wireless networks, but often this software isn't very good. You'll also have to turn to the wireless adaptor's manual to find out how to use it.

A better way is to force Windows to take control over a network adaptor. This can be done in several ways. First, a lot of client software can be turned off by right-clicking the icon in the Notification Area and selecting an option. This is usually along the lines of Let Windows manage this connection or Disable client software.

You may still have problems with Windows displaying a message that it can't manage a wireless connection, though. This can be easily fixed. In XP, right-click on the wireless icon in the Notification Area and select Open Network Connections. Double-click the wireless network connection, select Properties, click the wireless networks tab and choose Use Windows to configure my wireless network settings.

In Vista, it's a little harder. Click on the Start menu and type cmd. Right-click on cmd.exe and select Run as administrator, selecting OK in the dialog boxes that appear. At the command line, type netsh wlan show settings.

Make a note of the name of the interface on the final line (probably Wireless Network Connection). Type netsh wlan set autoconfig enabled=yes interface="*name of the interface you noted down*". This should let you manage your wireless card through Windows.

Troubleshooting hardware problems

PCs ARE FINICKY beasts that seem to thrive on causing their owners trouble by not working properly. If you've followed our instructions all the way through but are still not happy with the way your computer works, don't panic.

The vast majority of problems are best solved by trying one fix at a time. After each attempted fix, try and run your PC again to see if the problem has been solved. This is better than trying several things at once, as you'll be able to track down what the problem is, which could be useful if your computer has similar difficulties later on.

The other thing to remember is that a lot of problems are caused by something simple, such as cables being plugged in the wrong way round, so check the simple stuff first before you start taking your computer apart.

We'll go through all the common problems that might affect your PC and suggest fixes that should get your system running. Before we start, though, you should never rule out simple problems, such

as a blown fuse or faulty cables. Changing power or internal cables can often solve a problem quickly and with little hassle.

While our suggestions are general, if you get a specific error message, you should make a note of it. From another computer, either yours or a friend's, type this message into a search engine. This should help you narrow down the problem. If these can't help you, then jump to the relevant chapter of this book for more in-depth guidance.

Finally, if your PC stops working just after you've installed some new hardware, remove it and turn your computer back on. If this fixes the problem, you can try and install the device again. If you still don't have any luck, then the problem probably lies with your new hardware and you should ask for a refund or replacement.

PC WON'T TURN ON
One of the most frustrating problems you can have with a PC is that it won't turn on. However, this

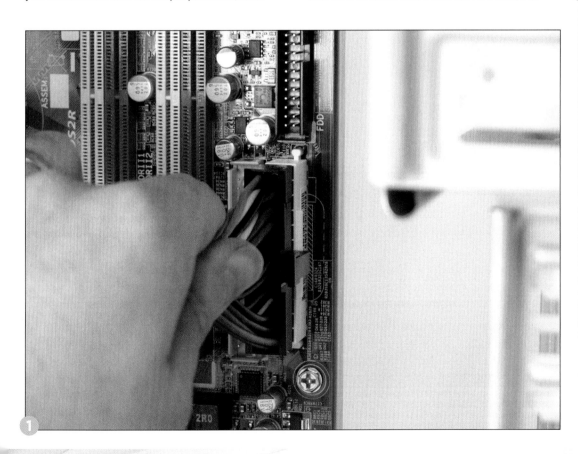

1 Make sure the power switch is connected to the motherboard

problem is usually easily fixed. First, check that you've got the power cable plugged in all the way and that the wall socket and power switch on the power supply are turned on. If that doesn't fix the problem, you'll need to open up your PC and have a look inside.

First, check that the case's power button is connected to the motherboard's power switch jumper. You'll need to check your motherboard's manual to find the exact pins to which it's supposed to be connected.

The other main reason that a computer won't start is because the power cables haven't been connected to the motherboard correctly. Make sure that the ATX power connector (the large 24-pin connector) is plugged into its socket and the secondary power connector is also connected (see page 123 for more details).

If you're still not having any luck, reseat the processor (see page 136), check that the memory is in the right slots and connected properly (page 138), and, if fitted, the graphics card (page 141). Finally, remove any expansion cards you've fitted.

If your computer still won't turn on, try removing the graphics card and the memory. If your PC turns on it will now beep at you (see page 32 for more information) to warn you that there's a problem. Refit the memory and try again.

If you still haven't found the source of the trouble, try using one stick of memory at a time to find out if one of them is causing the problem. You could also try removing the graphics card and any other expansion cards one at time.

WHAT'S THAT NOISE?
A more common scenario is that your computer will turn on, but you'll either get a blank screen or hear some beeps. The number of beeps is designed to tell you what the problem is. Unfortunately, your motherboard's manual won't explain these codes. However, our guide to BIOS beep codes on page 32 has a list of the common codes and the problems to which they relate. The manual for your motherboard should tell you which company manufactures the BIOS you're using, so you'll be able look up the appropriate codes in our guide.

The beeps from your BIOS can give you an idea of what's causing the problem, and you may think that the solution will probably entail replacing a faulty part in your computer. In our experience, however, this is rarely the case, and the fault is normally caused by devices not being connected properly.

You should always check that your memory, processor, hard disk, optical drive and power connectors are all in place before you start worrying about getting a replacement. Try installing one stick of memory at time, in case a faulty module is causing problems.

Sometimes faults can be caused by the motherboard not detecting your hardware correctly, particularly the processor. The easiest way to get it to do this is to reset the CMOS, which wipes the BIOS back to its default state. This should force it to detect your hardware correctly and can solve a lot of problems. Our guide on page 122 will show you how to do this.

In general, most motherboards have a jumper that has to be placed over two pins to reset the CMOS. To reset it, you need to change the jumper and turn the PC on. Then turn the computer off and put the jumper back to its original setting. Some motherboards designed for overclocking have a dedicated button on the back. Hold this in and press the power button. Turn your PC off, take your finger off the button and turn your computer back on.

When you reset your CMOS, you'll be prompted by a warning message to hit F1 when your PC starts. Doing this will reset all the BIOS settings back to their default values. You'll now be able to follow our instructions on page 102 to configure your BIOS properly.

1 Resetting the CMOS can fix lots of hardware errors. The jumper pins are highlighted

2 Make sure your memory is correctly seated or you could get intermittent errors

ERROR MESSAGE ON STARTUP

When computers are first turned on they run a Power On Self Test (POST) to check that hardware is working correctly. This will identify if your processor isn't working processor, the keyboard isn't connected or memory isn't working.

Read any message carefully and then check the component that's at fault to make sure that it's plugged in correctly. In the case of memory, you should try installing one stick of RAM at a time to make sure that there's not a fault in one of the modules.

DRIVE TROUBLE

If your optical drive isn't being detected, make sure that it's connected properly. This is easy for SATA drives, as you just need to check the cable. For IDE drives, check the cable and the jumpers on the back. If you only have one optical drive, it should be set to master; if you have two, one should be set to master and one to slave.

You should also check that the IDE cable is inserted the right way round on both the drive and the motherboard. If your cable doesn't have a notch in it, then the red cable needs to be next to the power connector on the drive; on the motherboard, the red cable needs to be plugged

into pin 1 (this will be marked on the board or, at least, in the motherboard's manual).

For hard disks, make sure that the cable is connected properly. The easiest first step is to go into your computer's BIOS and restore it back to its default settings. To do this, you need to access your BIOS by pressing a certain key (usually Delete or F2) when your computer boots. Your motherboard's manual will explain how to do this, but look out for an onscreen message that will tell you which key to press when you first turn your computer on. Check the manual to find out how to access the hard disk screen. Our guide to the BIOS on page 102 tells you how to configure your disks correctly.

If your hard disk still isn't being detected, make sure that it's plugged into the right SATA port and not one that's designed for RAID. If all else fails, you may have a broken hard disk. Put your ear to the disk when it turns on; if you repeatedly hear a clunking noise, then it's probably broken.

CRASHING AT STARTUP

Perhaps the most frustrating problem is when your PC turns on correctly and recognises all your hardware but crashes without warning when you try to start Windows. We've seen this happen on

○

lots of computers, and the solution is to check your hardware methodically. The first step is to go into your BIOS and reset it back to default values. When you get into your BIOS, you need to find the section that lets you load default values. Often this is under the Exit menu, but this differs between manufacturers, so check your manual.

If you have the choice, try and load the Optimal default first, and the Fail-Safe default second. If you don't have these options, the basic default setting is best. Select Exit Saving Changes and your computer will restart. You may need to set up your BIOS the way you want it again by following our advice on page 102.

Typically, these kinds of problems are usually caused by just a few components. Overheating is one of the main causes, especially in the case of the processor. It's worth checking that your processor cooler is fitted properly (see page 136).

1 Resetting the BIOS back to its default settings can fix a lot of problems

2 Bad memory can cause lots of problems in PCs, including random Windows crashes. Memtest can help you track down the problem by running diagnostic tests on your RAM

This is particularly true of Intel processors, as the four push-in feet don't always go in smoothly. It's easy to miss one and end up with the cooler not making proper contact with the processor. Also check that the processor has an adequate covering of thermal paste, applying more where necessary.

If that doesn't do the job, the memory could be the culprit. Running an application such as Memtest86+ (see page 128) can help you test your memory and find any errors. If this application won't run, then it's worth manually checking your memory. First, make sure all the modules are seated properly in the correct sockets (page 138).

If you're still having trouble, then it may be that one stick of memory is causing the problem. Remove all but one stick and try it again. Swap the stick of memory for another one and try your computer again. By a process of elimination, you should be able to work out which stick of memory, if any, is damaged.

Other hardware can also cause problems, so it's worth checking that your hard disk (page 139) and optical drive (page 140) are connected properly. For the hard disk, make sure that it's connected to the right SATA port on your computer by checking your motherboard's manual. Some boards have ports that are reserved for RAID.

It could be that your hard disk or operating system file is damaged. Try performing a Windows repair installation (see page 112 for Vista and page 116 for Windows XP). If the installer won't load, it's possible that the hard disk is damaged and unable to be detected properly. Try unplugging the hard disk. If this allows the installer to run, you can run Hitachi's free Drive Fitness Test (page 130) to see if you can identify a fault with the hard disk. You can also try connecting the hard disk to a different SATA port. Finally, remove all non-essential hardware such as wireless adaptors and TV tuners one at a time to see if this fixes the problem. We've even seen times where an iPod plugged into a USB port stopped Windows from loading.

STARTING IN SAFE MODE
Try and start your computer in Safe Mode by tapping F8 when your computer powers on and then selecting Safe Mode. If this doesn't work, you've got a hardware fault and should follow our boot problems chapter (page 26). If Safe Mode does work, uninstall any software that you've recently installed (see page 13). Finally, try System Restore (see page 12).

If you still have no luck, you should try and restore a backup of your computer (page 84). Our chapters on boot problems (page 26) and Windows problems (page 34) should be able to help.

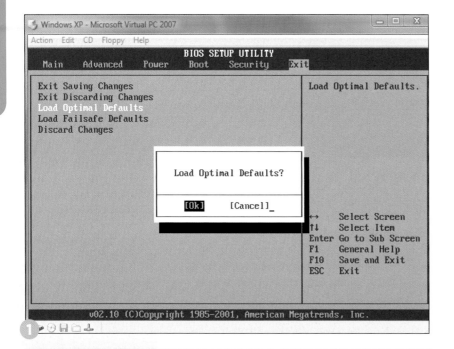

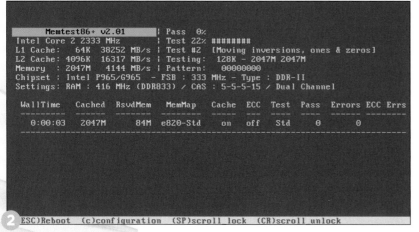

TRY COMPUTER SHOPPER
WITH 3 ISSUES FOR £1

As a technology enthusiast you already know how satisfying it is to get the most from your PC. Why not save time and effort when it comes to looking for new products and software by adding the **UK's best-selling computer magazine** to your monthly read?

Computer Shopper puts you in a great position to negotiate when buying anything to do with PCs. Every issue features **more industry advertisers then any other PC magazine**. So you can compare prices quickly and easily, to make sure you get the best deal.

Find out more with for 3 issues for £1

Right now you can claim the next 3 issues for just £1! It's a 100% risk free offer because if after 3 issues you're not completely satisfied you can write to cancel your subscription and you **won't pay any more than the £1 already debited**.

YOUR GREAT DEAL

- **3 issues for £1** to start your subscription
- If you're not satisfied, simply cancel and **pay no more than the £1** already debited
- **Save up to 26%** on the shop price
- **FREE delivery** to your door
- Get every issue **before it hits the shops**

CALL NOW ON **0844 844 0031**

Order securely online at **www.dennismags.co.uk/computershopper** entering offer code G0905CRM or return the invitation below

---

COMPUTER SHOPPER 3 ISSUES FOR £1 OFFER [UK ONLY]

YES! Please start my subscription to Computer Shopper with **3 issues for £1.** I understand that if I'm not completely satisfied, I can write to cancel during my introductory period and pay no more than the £1 already debited. To keep receiving Computer Shopper, I don't have to do anything – my subscription will automatically continue at the LOW RATE shown. The 3 issues for £1 are mine to keep, whatever I decide.

YOUR DETAILS – Please complete in BLOCK CAPITALS

MRS/MS
FORENAME

SURNAME

ADDRESS

POSTCODE

HOME PHONE
YEAR OF BIRTH

TEL NO.

Details will be processed by Dennis Publishing Ltd (publishers of Computer Shopper magazine) and our suppliers in full accordance with UK data protection legislation. Dennis Publishing Ltd may contact you with information about our other products and services. Please tick if you prefer NOT to receive such information by post ☐ phone ☐ mobile phone messaging ☐. Dennis Publishing Ltd occasionally shares data, on a secure basis, with other reputable companies that wish to contact you with information about their products and services. Please tick if you prefer NOT to receive such information by post ☐ phone ☐ Please tick if you DO wish to receive such information by email ☐ mobile phone messaging ☐. If the recipient of this subscription is under 18 please tick here ☐.

Direct Debit Payment – 3 issues for £1, then £21.99 every 6 issues (SAVE 26%)

Dennis Instruction to your Bank or Building Society to pay by Direct Debit **DIRECT Debit**

Please complete and send to: Freepost RLZS-ETGT-BCZR, Dennis Publishing Ltd, 800 Guillat Ave, Kent Science Park, Sittingbourne ME9 8GU

Name and full postal address of your Bank or Building Society

To the manager: Bank name

Address

Postcode

Account in the name(s) of

Branch sort code

Bank/Building Society account number

Originator's Identification Number

7	2	4	6	8	0

Ref no. to be completed by Dennis Publishing

Instructions to your bank or Building Society
Please pay Dennis Publishing Ltd. Direct Debits from the account detailed in this instruction subject to the safeguards assured by the Direct Debit Guarantee. I understand that this instruction may remain with Dennis Publishing Ltd and, if so, details will be passed electronically to my Bank/Building Society.

Signature(s)

Date

Banks and building societies may not accept Direct Debit instructions for some types of account

You will be able to view and amend your subscription details online at: www.subsinfo.co.uk

PLEASE RETURN TO:
Freeport RLZS-ETGT-BCZR, Computer Shopper Subscriptions, 800 Guillat Avenue, Kent Science Park, Sittingbourne ME9 8GU

Offer Code: G0905CRM

Chapter 2

Solving boot problems

IT'S RARE THAT you'll come across a boot-up problem that you can't fix yourself in a matter of minutes. You merely need to know how to go about diagnosing the problem.

In this chapter we'll explain what to do in common situations when your PC refuses to whir into life, when there are beeps emanating from its innards and when there's no image on your screen despite the PC appearing to work. Over the page you'll find our top 10 tips for solving boot problems, and on page 30 there's a handy flow chart, which should enable you to find your problem and resolve it quickly. Finally in this chapter, a list of common BIOS beep codes can be found on page 32.

Top 10 TIPS for solving boot problems

THERE ARE MANY reasons why a PC won't boot into its operating system. Many are easy to cure, while others take a little more time. Here are our top 10 tips for solving the vast majority of boot problems and getting Windows back up and running with the minimum of hassle.

1 **CHECK YOUR USB DEVICES**
USB devices are often the cause of PCs refusing to load Windows. The boot sequence appears to be running correctly, but just before you see the Windows splash screen, the PC appears to hang or freeze. You'll either see a black screen, or a white cursor flashing in the top-left corner of the screen. Usually this is caused by USB devices, particularly memory card readers. Check whether you've left a flash drive in a USB port or a memory card in a reader (or digital camera or camcorder) that's connected to your PC. Many printers also have memory card readers. Remove any cards you find and press your PC's reset button to reboot it. Windows should now load properly.

2 **CHECK FOR OPTICAL DISCS**
It's easy to leave a bootable CD or DVD in a drive accidentally. This could cause your PC to refuse to boot, or to boot into an application other than your operating system. It may not be obvious that your PC is booting from an optical disc, so check that your drives are empty and reboot.

3 **CHECK THE BOOT ORDER**
BIOS settings are critical for booting, so if you see a message such as "NTLDR is missing. Press Ctrl+Alt+Del to restart" you should enter the BIOS and check the boot sequence. When you see the POST screen, press Del (some computers will require you to press F2, F10 or F12, but most display a message telling you which key to press). Look for an Advanced BIOS Options menu and a Boot Sequence menu within that. Ensure that the primary boot device is the hard disk that has your operating system on it. If you have more than one hard disk and don't know which one Windows is on, you may have to try setting each as the primary device and rebooting to see if it fixes the problem. CD-ROM and floppy drives can boot before the hard disk, but this will slow the boot time down.

4 **CHECK FOR STRANGE NOISES**
Listen for any unusual noises coming from your PC. As your PC boots, you should hear flurries of clicking from the hard disk, but if there's a rhythmic scraping or chirping noise, your hard disk may have failed. In this case, turn to page 84 to find out how to restore a backup to a new disk.

5 **CHECK YOUR CABLES**
Make sure that no cables have become dislodged. Start with power cables and both ends of your monitor's cable. If you don't find any

Sidebar notes

1 Make sure you disconnect any USB devices if Windows isn't loading properly

2 Overheating can cause the dreaded 'blue screen of death'

3 If you see a message such as this, you should check the boot order in the BIOS

4 Check the power cables if your graphics card is emitting a high-pitched noise

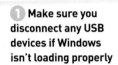

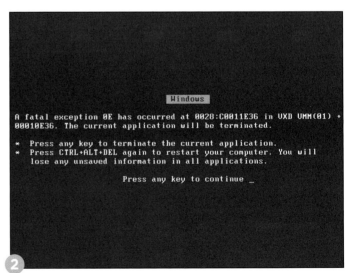

```
NTLDR is missing
Press Ctrl+Alt+Del to restart
_
```

problems, remove your PC's side panel and check internal cables, particularly the hard disk's power and data cables. Many modern graphics cards require one or two power cables, so check these are properly connected. Without a power cable, some graphics cards emit a high-pitched noise.

6 RESET THE BIOS

Overclocking can cause boot problems, so you should check your motherboard's manual to see if there's a way to boot the PC at standard speeds without losing all your BIOS settings. If not, you'll need to reset the BIOS (this is also known as resetting the CMOS). The same manual should document the procedure, which usually involves moving a motherboard jumper to a reset position, although in rare cases you may find a switch or button on the outside of the PC.

7 CHECK FOR OVERHEATING

Your PC may be overheating and it may fail to boot after an unexplained 'blue screen'. Wait for at least 30 minutes to allow the components to cool down and try turning on the PC again. Meanwhile, investigate potential reasons for overheating, such as a broken fan. You should ensure that your PC isn't placed next to a heat source such as a radiator.

8 BEEP BEEP!

If your PC is making an unusual beeping noise, you'll need to refer to your motherboard manual to diagnose the problem. If you don't have a manual, we've provided a list of common BIOS beep codes on page 32. Some motherboards have LED displays that you can use along with the descriptions of each code in the manual to determine the status of the POST sequence. These often make it much simpler to solve the problem as you can see precisely how far the PC makes it through the boot process before failing. Knowing this information should make it obvious which component is causing the problem.

9 CHECK HARDWARE AND SOFTWARE

If you've recently installed a piece of hardware and you see a blue screen when your PC boots, the cause is probably the new hardware. Uninstall it and see if it fixes the problem. It could also be caused by new software, so try and boot into Safe Mode by pressing F8 repeatedly after the initial POST screen. It's also worth noting that you'll probably see a blue screen if you've recently swapped the hard disk for one from a different PC and tried to boot from it.

10 UNPLUG YOUR HARDWARE

If none of the tips above has helped you solve the problem, you should disconnect any unnecessary hardware. All a PC needs to show a POST message is a motherboard, a processor, one memory module, a graphics card and a power supply. All other hardware can be unplugged. If the PC now boots, begin reconnecting other components one at a time until the problem returns. If it still doesn't boot, it's likely to be a hardware failure. At this point, it's worth trying to borrow components known to be working, and swapping them with yours to find out which of the core parts is defective.

Fixing boot problems

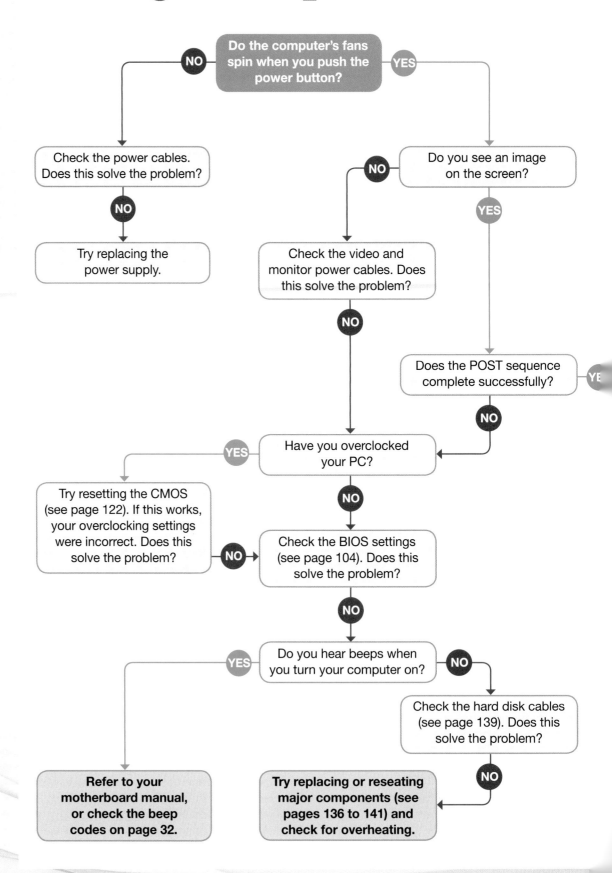

Do the computer's fans spin when you push the power button?

NO → Check the power cables. Does this solve the problem?
NO → Try replacing the power supply.

YES → Do you see an image on the screen?

NO → Check the video and monitor power cables. Does this solve the problem?

YES → Does the POST sequence complete successfully?

YES

NO → Have you overclocked your PC?

YES → Try resetting the CMOS (see page 122). If this works, your overclocking settings were incorrect. Does this solve the problem?

NO → Check the BIOS settings (see page 104). Does this solve the problem?

NO → Do you hear beeps when you turn your computer on?

YES → Refer to your motherboard manual, or check the beep codes on page 32.

NO → Check the hard disk cables (see page 139). Does this solve the problem?

NO → Try replacing or reseating major components (see pages 136 to 141) and check for overheating.

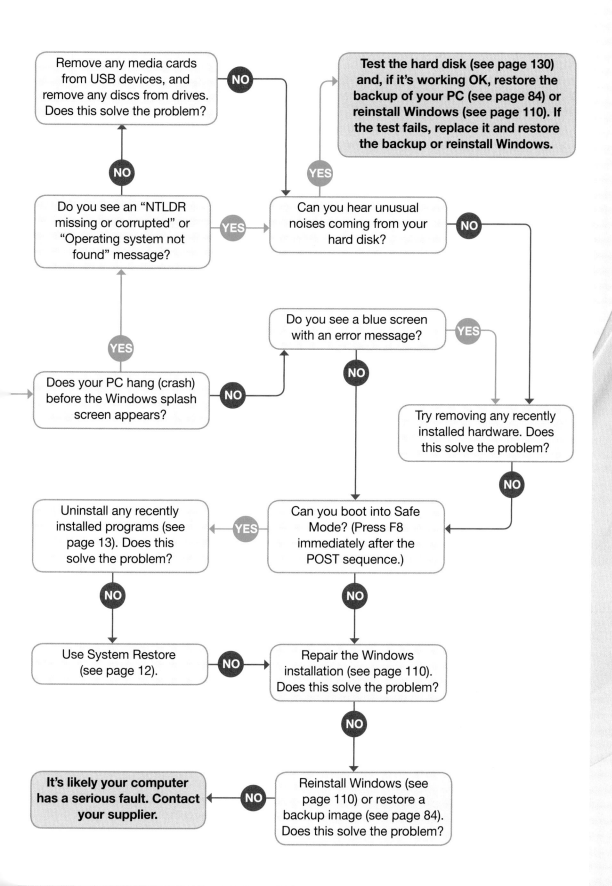

Remove any media cards from USB devices, and remove any discs from drives. Does this solve the problem?

NO

NO

Do you see an "NTLDR missing or corrupted" or "Operating system not found" message?

YES

Can you hear unusual noises coming from your hard disk?

YES

Test the hard disk (see page 130) and, if it's working OK, restore the backup of your PC (see page 84) or reinstall Windows (see page 110). If the test fails, replace it and restore the backup or reinstall Windows.

NO

YES

Does your PC hang (crash) before the Windows splash screen appears?

NO

Do you see a blue screen with an error message?

YES

NO

Try removing any recently installed hardware. Does this solve the problem?

NO

Uninstall any recently installed programs (see page 13). Does this solve the problem?

YES

Can you boot into Safe Mode? (Press F8 immediately after the POST sequence.)

NO

NO

Use System Restore (see page 12).

NO

Repair the Windows installation (see page 110). Does this solve the problem?

NO

It's likely your computer has a serious fault. Contact your supplier.

NO

Reinstall Windows (see page 110) or restore a backup image (see page 84). Does this solve the problem?

BIOS beep codes

WHEN YOU SWITCH on or reset your PC it performs a diagnostic test called a Power-On Self Test (POST) to check that all the components are present and working correctly.

First, it checks core components such as the system clock, processor, RAM, keyboard controller and graphics card. If any device fails this part of the POST, you'll hear series of beeps from the PC. After the graphics card has passed its test, the BIOS can then indicate any errors onscreen, such as the classic "Keyboard error or no keyboard present. Press F1 to continue" message.

When the POST has completed successfully, most PCs emit a short beep to let you know the hardware is working correctly. However, beep codes differ depending on the BIOS manufacturer, so refer to your motherboard manual if you have it. Below are some common beep codes for popular BIOSes. If you're unsure which BIOS your PC has, try to match the sequence of beeps with the codes.

AMI BIOS

- **ONE BEEP** All OK
- **TWO BEEPS** Memory parity error (reseat or replace memory)
- **THREE BEEPS** Memory read or write error (reseat or replace memory)
- **FOUR BEEPS** Motherboard timer problem (replace motherboard)
- **FIVE BEEPS** Processor or memory error (reseat or replace processor and memory)
- **SIX BEEPS** Keyboard controller failure (replace motherboard)

- **SEVEN BEEPS** Processor exception interrupt error (reseat or replace processor)
- **EIGHT BEEPS** Display memory read or write failure (reseat or replace graphics card)
- **NINE BEEPS** ROM checksum error (replace BIOS chip or motherboard)
- **10 BEEPS** CMOS shutdown read or write error (replace BIOS chip or motherboard)
- **11 BEEPS** Bad cache memory (replace cache memory if possible)
- **ONE LONG, THREE SHORT BEEPS** Memory error (reseat or remove any memory recently added and reseat all other memory)
- **ONE LONG, EIGHT SHORT BEEPS** Graphics card error (reseat graphics card)

AWARD BIOS

- **ONE LONG, TWO SHORT BEEPS** Graphics card error (reseat or replace graphics card)
- **ONE LONG, THREE SHORT BEEPS** No graphics card, or graphics memory error (install or replace graphics card)
- **TWO SHORT BEEPS** Memory error (reseat or replace memory)
- **ONE HIGH-PITCHED BEEP** Processor overheating
- **ONE HIGH-PITCHED BEEP, ONE LOW-PITCHED BEEP** Processor error

PHOENIX BIOS

Phoenix BIOSes produce a series of beeps separated by a pause. For example:
beep… beep beep beep… beep… beep would be 1-3-1-1

- **1-1-4-1** Level 2 cache error (reseat or replace the processor)
- **1-2-2-3** BIOS ROM checksum (replace BIOS chip or motherboard)
- **1-3-1-1** Memory refresh test failure (reseat or replace memory)
- **1-3-1-3** Keyboard controller failure (replace the motherboard)
- **1-3-4-1** Memory failure (reseat or replace memory)
- **1-3-4-3** Memory refresh test failure (reseat or replace memory)
- **1-4-1-1** Memory refresh test failure (reseat or replace memory)
- **2-1-2-3** BIOS error (replace BIOS chip or motherboard)
- **2-2-3-1** IRQ problem (remove expansion cards or replace motherboard)

1 Your PC may be sending you a message when it's booting up

Chapter 3

Solving Windows problems

AS WE SHOWED in the previous chapter, fixing problems that prevent your PC booting up is relatively straightforward, but problems that cause Windows to crash or run slowly can be more difficult to identify and rectify.

However, as well as application error messages and codes, there are several tools built into Windows that should help you figure out what's going wrong. Over the next few pages, we'll introduce the Device Manager, the Task Manager and the Event Viewer, all of which can provide valuable information for problem-solving.

Before you begin, you'll need to work out which tool will be most helpful for your problem, so turn the page and use the flowchart to find the symptoms and the possible cause.

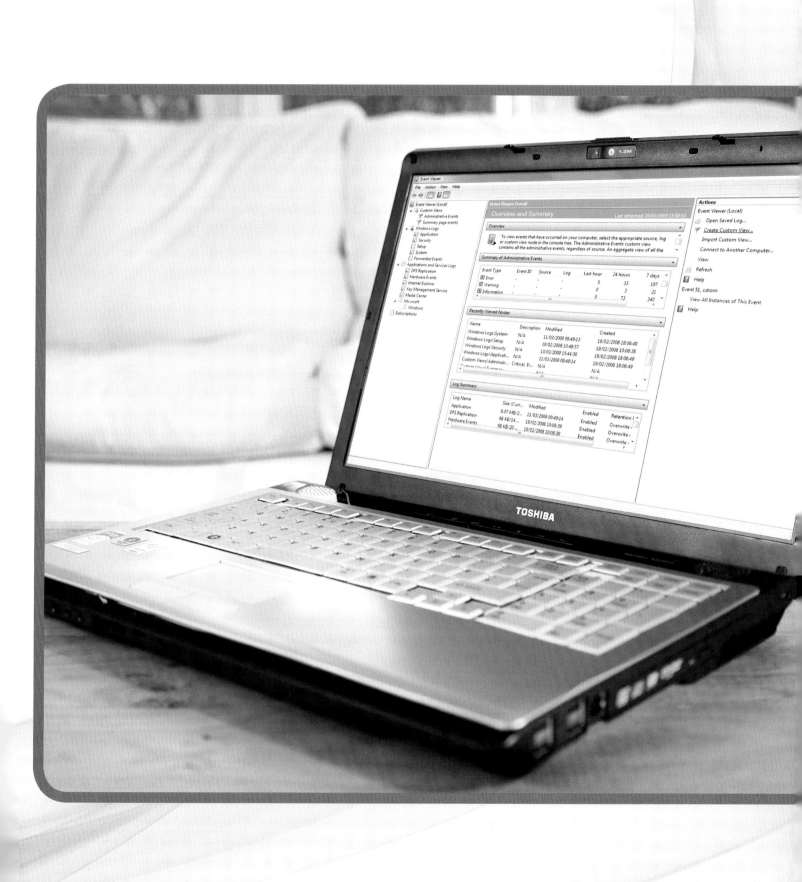

Windows problems

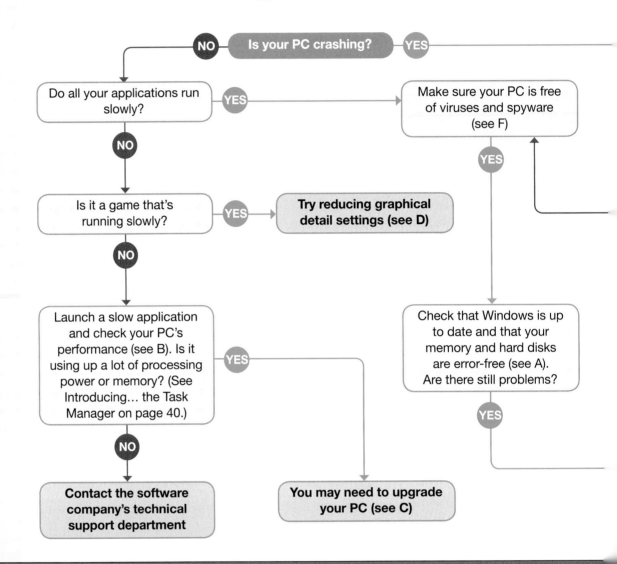

Is your PC crashing?

Do all your applications run slowly?

Make sure your PC is free of viruses and spyware (see F)

Is it a game that's running slowly?

Try reducing graphical detail settings (see D)

Launch a slow application and check your PC's performance (see B). Is it using up a lot of processing power or memory? (See Introducing... the Task Manager on page 40.)

Check that Windows is up to date and that your memory and hard disks are error-free (see A). Are there still problems?

Contact the software company's technical support department

You may need to upgrade your PC (see C)

THE A TO G OF FIXING YOUR PC

A Test your memory using Memtest, which you can download for free (see page 128). If it finds any errors, you may need to replace some of your PC's RAM. Contact your PC's technical support line. It's also worth checking that your hard disk has no errors by using the error-checking tool in Windows (see page 88). Just right-click on the drive, choose Properties and click the Tool tab. Press the Check Now button.

Finally, make sure that Windows has the latest updates. Open Automatic Updates in the Windows Security Center, which is available in the Control Panel.

B If an application is running slowly, it's worth finding out how much of your computer's processing power and memory it is using.

Close all your other applications and press Ctrl-Alt-Del simultaneously to open the Windows Task Manager (see page 40). In the Processes tab you'll be able to see what percentage of your processor power and how much memory (divide by 1,000 for a rough figure in megabytes) each program is using. If it's hogging all the processing power or most of your RAM and is still slow, your PC is struggling with this program.

C If your application needs more system resources, you may need to upgrade your PC. If you're short on memory, an upgrade is relatively simple. Check your manual to see what kind of memory your PC accepts or go to *www.crucial.com* and use the online system scanner.

D Modern games can be incredibly demanding. If your graphics card is struggling, it will produce a low frame rate, which causes the game to pause and stutter. Run the game and find the graphics settings in the options menu.

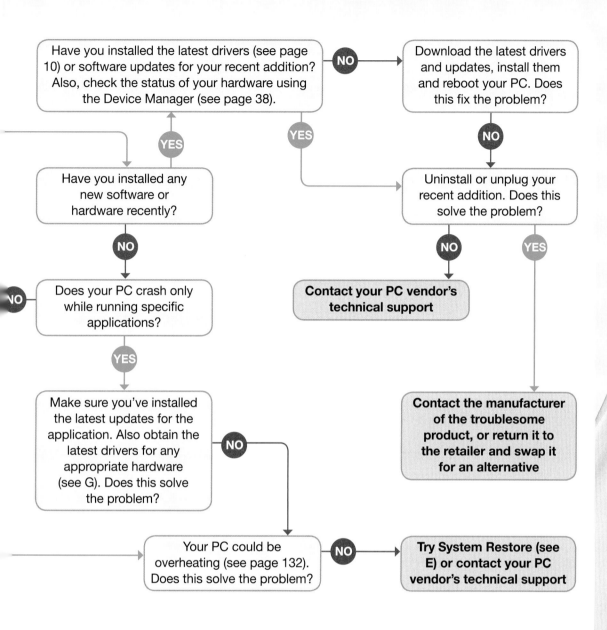

Have you installed the latest drivers (see page 10) or software updates for your recent addition? Also, check the status of your hardware using the Device Manager (see page 38).

NO → Download the latest drivers and updates, install them and reboot your PC. Does this fix the problem?

YES

Have you installed any new software or hardware recently?

NO

Does your PC crash only while running specific applications?

YES

NO

Uninstall or unplug your recent addition. Does this solve the problem?

NO → **Contact your PC vendor's technical support**

YES

Make sure you've installed the latest updates for the application. Also obtain the latest drivers for any appropriate hardware (see G). Does this solve the problem?

NO

Contact the manufacturer of the troublesome product, or return it to the retailer and swap it for an alternative

Your PC could be overheating (see page 132). Does this solve the problem?

NO → **Try System Restore (see E) or contact your PC vendor's technical support**

Try turning off anti-aliasing (AA) and anisotropic filtering (AF) first to see if this improves your frame rate. If not, reduce the resolution to 1,024x768 or lower.

Make sure that you have the latest patches for your game and the latest drivers for your graphics card by going to Nvidia's or ATI's website, or check your laptop manufacturer's site if you have built-in graphics.

E Your PC keeps a record of any changes made to its settings. If you encounter a problem, you can restore the settings from an earlier date. In Windows

XP, the System Restore tool is under Programs, Accessories, System Tools. Vista users can simply type System Restore into Vista's search box. Follow the instructions to restore your PC to the state it was in before your problem started.

F Slow performance may be a sign that your PC is running some undesirable software. This can include such nasties as viruses, privacy-invading spyware and aggravating advertising pop-ups. These programs can be grouped together under the term malicious software (or malware, for short).

Run a virus scan to find any malware on your PC. If you don't have anti-virus software, download AVG Free Edition from *http://free.avg.com* and run a full scan.

G If certain types of program such as games cause your PC to crash, check that you have the latest drivers for any hardware that's responsible for running them. Update your graphics card drivers if your PC crashes when playing games or video; update sound card drivers to solve audio playback troubles; and find new TV tuner drivers for any TV card-related problems.

Introducing... the Device Manager

THE DEVICE MANAGER allows you to view all the hardware inside your computer. It's also the place to go when you're having problems with hardware, as it can help diagnose faults and update device drivers. To open the Device Manager in Vista, go to the Control Panel, System and Maintenance, Device Manager. In Windows XP, it's the same procedure, but the Control Panel icon is simply called System. It's quicker to right-click on My Computer, then Properties, then Device Manager.

DEVICE SQUAD

You may never have visited the Device Manager before, as there's usually no reason to. When you install a piece of new hardware, you'll also install any drivers from CD. This process automatically copies files to the appropriate places and the hardware is added to the Device Manager list.

Although you can enable and disable hardware from the Device Manager, it's often more convenient to do so from other places in Windows. The same is true for updating drivers. While you can manually initiate a driver update from an item's properties page in the Device Manager, there's usually no need to, since most drivers downloaded from manufacturers' websites automatically remove old versions and install the new ones.

However, when your hardware stops working as it should or you can't automatically update drivers, the Device Manager comes into its own. The default view of devices by type shows a collapsed tree structure, where just the headings are shown,

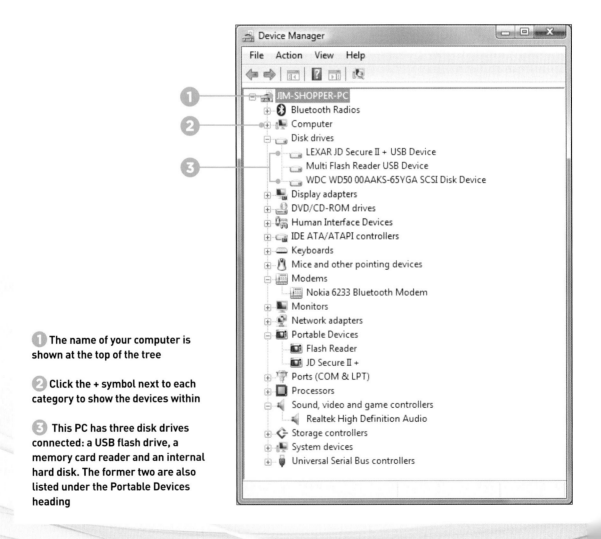

1 The name of your computer is shown at the top of the tree

2 Click the + symbol next to each category to show the devices within

3 This PC has three disk drives connected: a USB flash drive, a memory card reader and an internal hard disk. The former two are also listed under the Portable Devices heading

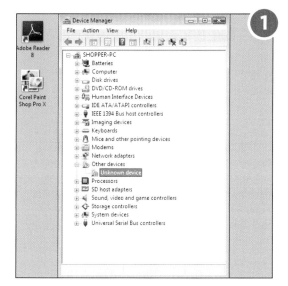

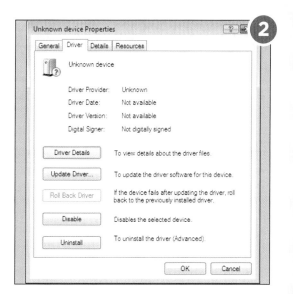

but it will automatically expand any category that contains a problem. You may see a yellow exclamation mark next to a component's name, or a red cross (in XP) or an arrow pointing downwards (in Vista). The exclamation mark might mean that the hardware drivers aren't installed, or that the hardware itself cannot start. A red cross or arrow denotes that the hardware is disabled.

Here we'll assume that your Windows desktop is showing huge icons and you can't adjust the resolution in the Display Settings dialog.

① OPEN THE DEVICE MANAGER
Scan down the Device Manager list until you come to the Display adapters entry. Click the + symbol, and you should see an exclamation mark, which means the drivers aren't installed. If there's no Display adapters entry, look for Other devices, which should have Unknown device listed.

② CHECK THE DRIVER
Right-click on this, or on the name of the graphics card, and choose Properties. Click on the

Driver tab and you'll see details of the currently installed driver, if there is one. You may see Microsoft listed next to Driver Provider, but you should install the latest driver from your graphics card manufacturer, such as Nvidia, AMD or Intel.

③ DOWNLOAD THE NEW DRIVER
Visit the appropriate manufacturer's website to obtain the latest driver and download it. If necessary, unzip it into a folder on your hard disk. If the file is a self-executable – ending in .exe – you can run it at this point. If not, return to the Properties page you navigated to in Step 2, and click the Update Driver… button. Click the Browse my computer for driver software button.

④ INSTALL THE DRIVER
Click the Browse… button on the next window that appears. Navigate to the folder where you unzipped the drivers and click Next. Windows should install the drivers, and you may see the screen flicker during the process. You may also have to reboot your PC to finalise the installation. ◻

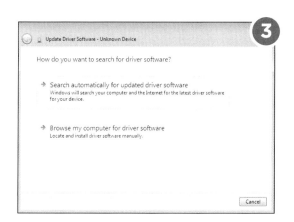

Introducing... the Task Manager

WHEN YOU ENCOUNTER a problem in Windows, your first stop should almost always be the Task Manager. This allows you to shut applications down, view system information – such as the load under which the processor and memory are working – and much more besides.

The Task Manager is particularly useful for identifying troublesome applications or services that are hogging your PC's resources, such as memory or processor time, and slowing it down. It can also help you monitor the size of Windows' page file, as well as keep tabs on network activity.

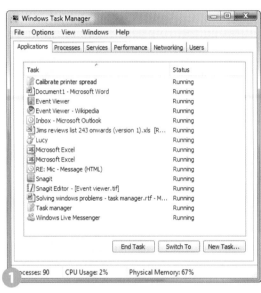

① **The Applications tab lets you view which applications are running, and allows you to shut them down**

② **The Processes tab shows a detailed list of all your programs**

③ **Vista's Services tab allows you to start, stop and configure system services such as Task Scheduler and WiFi configuration**

④ **The performance tab shows graphs of processor load and memory usage**

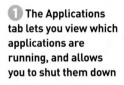

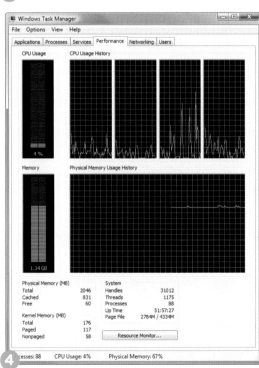

The fastest way to open the Task Manager in Windows XP and Windows Vista is to press the Ctrl-Shift-Esc keys at the same time. A window will open that sits on top of any existing windows, and will remain that way until you either minimise or close it.

The first tab shows the list of running applications. This is useful when an application won't shut down, as you can highlight it in the list and click the End Task button. If the application has crashed and you've been unable to save your work, forcing it to end will probably cause any changes since you last saved the file to be lost, unless the application has an auto-save or auto-recovery feature. For this reason, it's sometimes best to wait for programs that are not responding to come back to life rather than forcing them to quit. Any more than a few minutes of non-responsiveness, however, probably indicates that a program really has crashed.

PART OF THE PROCESS

The Processes tabs lists which programs are running in much greater detail, showing memory and processor usage. Processes using an unusually high amount of the processor or memory may be malfunctioning and may need to be ended and restarted. In many cases, an application listed in the Applications tab will translate to several processes, and you'll sometimes need to use the Processes tab when you can't end a program from the Applications tab. In XP, it's more difficult to determine what each process does, but Vista's Task Manager additionally shows a description of the process, although you may have to scroll right or expand the Description column to see it fully.

You can sort the list of processes by any column. A useful way to do this is by Owner. You'll see your username, plus any other users currently logged on, and 'system', which is the operating system's processes. You should be able to end any processes next to a username without a problem, except that the program or service will no longer function until you restart it or reboot. Ending system processes is more dangerous, as you might cause Windows to crash or stop working properly. However, the worst that will happen is you'll need to reboot your computer.

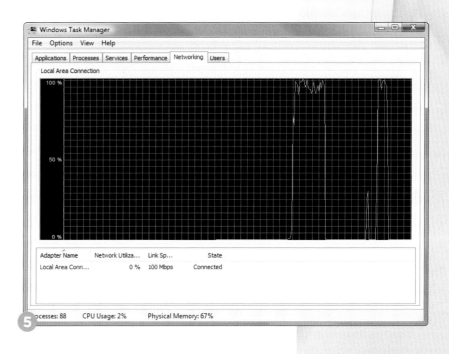

The beauty of the Processes tab is that you can choose additional columns of information. From the View menu, choose Select Columns… and you'll see a list of options. We'd recommend ticking I/O reads and I/O writes, as this shows which processes are thrashing the hard disk and memory. Any process that is constantly reading and/or writing could have a problem, and you should investigate it further by finding out what the process is for (see page 45 for more on diagnosing suspect processes).

Next in Vista is the Services tab. This is similar to the Processes tab, and lists each service's process ID (PID) which is often included in error messages. This can often help you identify troublesome services and end them.

The Performance tab shows several graphs: one for each processor core and one for page file usage. On the left you can see the current processor and page file usage. If either of these is very high, it could explain why Windows is running slowly. The reason could be because you're running a demanding application or an application has crashed. If you leave your computer in Sleep mode rather than turning it off, the page file size will build up and slow Windows down. A reboot should fix this issue.

5 You can see how much bandwidth is being used in the Networking tab

Introducing... the Event Viewer

THE EVENT VIEWER presents detailed system logs, which are special files that record significant events that happen on your computer, such as when an application encounters an error or when the computer enters a standby power state. It's similar to an aeroplane's black box recorder. It lets you see a summary of your PC's health, and can help you pinpoint which application has caused a problem, as well as providing error codes that can be useful for Google searches (see page 45 for more on error codes).

To launch Event Viewer, either type it into Vista's search bar, or right-click on Computer in the Start menu and choose Manage. Event Viewer is the second item in the System Tools list.

FINDING YOUR WAY AROUND

Although Vista's Event Viewer looks more user-friendly than XP's, it's still daunting for most people. It's really designed to assist technicians diagnose faults, but even the non-technical can glean useful information from it.

1 The Overview and Summary panel lets you see at a glance the number of errors and warnings

2 You can jump quickly to any of the logs using the tree in the left pane

3 The Actions pane on the right-hand side of the Event Viewer lets you quickly create custom views, as well as changing the view and refreshing the overview. Actions are context-sensitive, and change depending on the current view

If you know a particular application isn't working as it should, you can search for it in the Application log, which is listed under Windows Logs on the left. Let's say that Google's Updater application isn't working. Click on Application beneath Windows Logs and the listing will appear in the middle pane. You can scroll down the list until you see Google Update in the Source column. Highlight the event and you'll see the error details in the pane below. You may have to resize the window to see the full width of the description as it doesn't automatically wrap the text to fit.

The general description should explain the nature of the error; for example, a required component wasn't found or the installation is corrupted. In this case, reinstalling the application should fix the problem. You may also see a particular filename mentioned, which may help to identify the problem, and an error code, such as

Error: 0x80072ee2. Copying and pasting this into Google along with the application name may shed more light on the problem if the description doesn't make it obvious what you should do next.

SYSTEM LOG

The System log covers operating system events, and can be useful for diagnosing problems with hardware drivers. For example, your PC may be refusing to go into sleep mode or refusing to wake up from it. The System log may show warnings such as 'Display driver nvlddmnkm stopped responding'. This could indicate that it's your graphics card driver causing the problem, and that updating the driver may cure it.

Most of the log will likely contain Information entries, which tell you when services started and stopped. They may also give warnings, such as the one shown in the screen below: "Windows cannot store Bluetooth authentication codes on the local adapter. Bluetooth keyboards might not work in the system BIOS during startup." Again, this can explain why certain problems are occurring.

CUSTOM VIEWS

In Vista's Event Viewer, you can create custom views, which allow you to see relevant information more easily, instead of having to wade through thousands of entries in each log. To create a custom view, click Create Custom View… in the right-hand pane of the Event Viewer. You can then select what time period the view should cover, which event types to include, and how to filter them, whether by log or by source.

A simple custom view could filter the errors and warnings from the application and system logs over the previous 24 hours. When you name and save the custom view, it will appear in the Custom Views section in the left-hand pane.

1 The detailed information on each error can help you diagnose problems

2 This alert warns that Bluetooth keyboards may not work in the BIOS

3 Creating custom views is a good way to keep track of relevant information

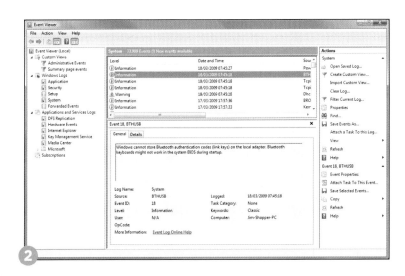

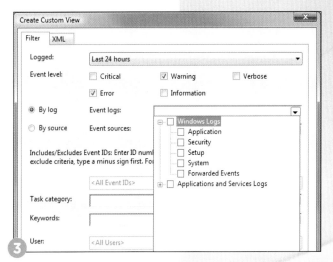

Introducing... the Reliability Monitor

THOSE WITH WINDOWS Vista have an extra troubleshooting tool on hand in the form of the Reliability Monitor. This is much more user-friendly than the Event Viewer (see page 42), but it doesn't give as many details.

To launch the Reliability Monitor, either type 'perf' into the Vista search bar or right-click on Computer in the Start menu and choose Manage. Reliability Monitor can be found under the Reliability and Performance heading in the Computer Management tree.

What's particularly useful about the Reliability Monitor is that it graphs reliability over time (with a stability rating of 0 to 10), so you can see at a glance when problems began to occur, and whether your computer is currently performing well or not. Below the graph, you can see which type of failures occurred on a particular date, and you can also track software installs and uninstalls.

To see the reliability report for a particular day, either click on the graph directly or choose the date from the drop-down box on the right of the graph. If more than 30 days' worth of information is stored, you can use the scroll bar at the bottom to view the section you want.

If you click on a day when there was an application failure (marked by a red circle with a white 'x' in the Application Failures row), you may see a message saying something like "Outlook.exe stopped working". This doesn't help you find the cause of the problem, but you could then check the Event Viewer's Application log on this date for more details.

Where the Reliability Monitor is useful is in tracking crashes after software installs or updates. If Windows – or an application such as Outlook or Internet Explorer – has been crashing for a week or two and you're not sure why, you can check the Reliability Monitor to see whether an update or another application was installed, which may be causing the problem.

KEEPING UP TO DATE

Our top tip is to keep your computer fully up to date with the latest Windows updates. Also, don't ignore pop-up update requests from applications and plugins, such as Adobe's Flash player for browsers. Finally, ensure that your graphics card drivers are kept up to date. Nvidia and AMD usually update drivers each month, and this can improve game reliability, especially for new titles.

Don't worry too much about the actual reliability figure shown by the graph. This is arguably a gimmick, and doesn't really tell you much. However, it's still quite satisfying to track down problems that are causing applications or Windows to crash and seeing the resulting rise in reliability over a few weeks.

1 Keep an eye on the Reliability Monitor over a week or two, and you should be able to get to the root of Windows problems

2 Click on a date to see information from that particular day

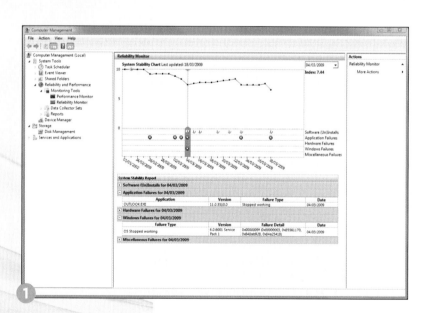

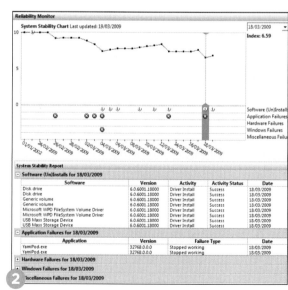

Error codes and messages

USUALLY WHEN APPLICATIONS crash, they lock up and won't respond to mouse clicks or the keyboard. This is often accompanied by a (Not Responding) message in the application's title bar, and can be incredibly frustrating, especially if you haven't saved your work. If the application won't respond after several minutes, you'll probably have to use the Task Manager (see page 40) to close it.

At other times you may see an error message or code. This may not mean much, even if you read the full description of the error, since Microsoft and other developers of Windows software don't generally design error messages to be understood by end users. Fortunately, you can harness the search power of Google to try to find out what the problem is and what you can do to fix it.

When you see an error message or code, note it down rather than simply dismissing the dialog box by clicking the OK or Ignore buttons. Sometimes you may be able to copy and paste the message directly from the screen. Then type or paste the code into Google's search box along with the name of the application or version of Windows, and scour the results for an explanation of the problem, and hopefully, the solution.

While this may sound a little imprecise, there's no more up-to-date resource than the internet for solving tricky problems. Someone is bound to have experienced the same error before you, no matter

how obscure you think it is, and may have posted a fix online. If you prefer to go straight to a website for answers, one of the best is *www.fixya.com*. Experts Exchange (*www.experts-exchange.com*) is better still, but costs $13 (around £8) per month.

Searching Google can also be beneficial if you have identified a process in the Task Manager (see page 40) that's making Windows run slowly. Make a note of the process's name and type it into the search box. The results should give you an idea of what the process does, and how to fix it.

1 Microsoft's Help and Support site and Google are good resources for interpreting error messages

5 TOP TIPS

1 If you're experiencing an error or unexpected application behaviour and haven't installed any hardware, software or updates recently, reboot your PC. This can often do the trick.

2 Try reinstalling the offending application. Uninstalling and reinstalling applications can repair problems that may have been caused by a virus or another application. Some programs have repair options that can be accessed from the Add/Remove programs list in Windows' Control Panel (this is called Programs and Features in Vista).

3 If you have a Windows error, search Microsoft's Help and Support website at *http://support.microsoft.com*. Click on the Error message link in the Get help with… menu. There are

thousands of solutions to errors here, and you may find that you need to download a patch from this website to fix your problem.

4 Uninstall any programs you're no longer using. Applications can be incompatible with one another, particularly if you have lots of programs that do a similar job, and it pays to keep your computer as lean as possible.

5 Keep Windows up to date with the latest patches. Make sure Windows Update is enabled by clicking on its icon in the Control Panel. You can tell Windows whether to download and install updates automatically, download them and let you install them at your convenience, or merely notify you that updates are available.

Chapter 4

Accessories

IT ISN'T ALWAYS your PC's base unit that suffers problems – peripherals can go wrong, too. Whether it's your monitor or printer, there are often quick fixes that will save you time as well as money calling a costly helpline.

In this chapter, you'll find tips on fixing common problems as well as more detailed help on troubleshooting a blank monitor screen and dodgy print-outs. We've also included a guide to the various monitor interfaces and compatible cables on page 52, plus help on sound problems on page 50, as this is one area that deserves separate treatment from general Windows problems.

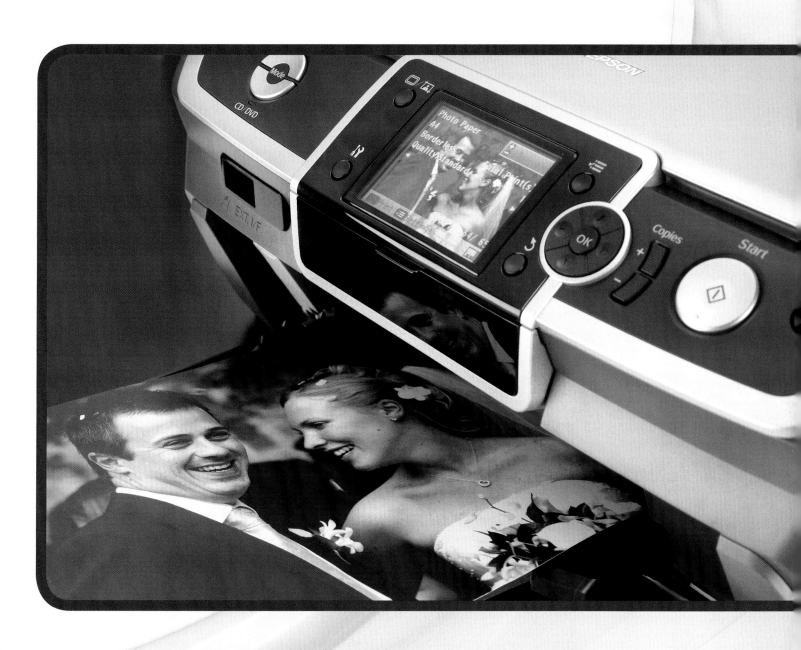

Top 10 TIPS for fixing peripheral problems

1 CHECK ALL CABLES

We've said it before, but it bears repeating: check your cables. Whatever problem you're having with your peripheral, make sure the cables are properly connected at both ends and that they're not damaged. If something won't turn on at all, check the fuse in the plug, as these do fail occasionally. Keep a couple of 3A and 13A fuses to hand so you can quickly swap out a suspect fuse.

2 TRY ANOTHER USB PORT

When USB peripherals aren't working properly or aren't being correctly detected by Windows, try unplugging the cable and plugging it into a different USB port. This forces Windows to redetect the hardware and reinstall the drivers, and often solves annoying problems.

If a peripheral isn't behaving properly, check if it's plugged into a USB hub. If it is, disconnect it and reconnect it to a port on your PC or laptop, as some devices, including Apple iPods, don't like being connected via a USB hub.

3 DRY IT OUT

If you accidentally spill liquid on any of your peripherals, unplug all their cables immediately. Place them somewhere hot and dry, such as an airing cupboard, for at least 24 hours to allow them to dry out. There's no guarantee this will save them, but it often works. If you spill a sticky liquid on a peripheral, don't be tempted to pour extra water on to flush it out – this could cause more damage. If it fails to work after the drying out

process, try disassembling it. Most warranties won't cover damage caused by spillages (but check first), so you have nothing to lose by disassembling a peripheral. Remote controls often benefit from being taken apart, as liquid can be trapped between the rubber membrane and the circuit board, preventing buttons from working.

4 PS/2 WARNING

Don't forget that PS/2 peripherals aren't hot-pluggable. If you forget to connect a PS/2 keyboard or mouse to your PC and you only realise when you see an error message during the POST sequence or when the device doesn't work in Windows, don't plug it in. Turn the PC off first, and then connect it, even if it means holding down the power button after booting into Windows. You won't cause any damage to Windows.

5 USE THE RIGHT PORT

A classic mistake is to reach behind your PC to plug in a USB device without looking and inadvertently insert it into the Ethernet port. USB plugs are exactly the same width as a network socket, which means it feels like you've inserted the USB cable correctly as the plug is held tightly in place. It's only when Windows refuses to detect the device that you're aware something's not working properly.

6 KNOW YOUR COLOURS

The same goes for audio connections, as sound cards tend to use minijack sockets for

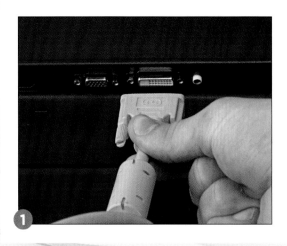

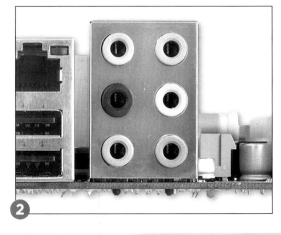

1 Make sure video cables are securely screwed in place

2 Know your sound card colours so you can connect the right cables to the right sockets

3 If you're having webcam problems, ensure your camera is properly selected in the application you're using it with

4 Eject your USB disks before unplugging them to avoid losing files

5 If your old CRT monitor stops working, it will be more cost-effective to buy a new one

everything and rarely have labels next to them. Here's a quick guide to the colour coding:

Green Main stereo output, usually used for front speakers or headphones
Pink Stereo microphone input
Light blue Stereo line input
Black Rear surround speakers
Orange Centre speaker and subwoofer output
Grey Middle surround speakers for 7.1 systems

7 CHECK WEBCAM SETTINGS

If you're having problems with your webcam, such as a lack of video, check the settings of the program that's using it (usually this will be an instant-messaging application such as Windows Live Messenger). Look for a webcam settings option in the menus and make sure you select the webcam from the list of video devices when asked.

If you don't see the make and model of the webcam listed, it may be because the drivers aren't properly installed. If reinstalling the latest drivers from the manufacturer's website doesn't solve the problem, try rebooting your PC and plugging the webcam into a different USB port.

8 ELIMINATING ECHOES

It's common to have problems with webcam audio. If you're using the webcam's built-in microphone, make sure it's selected correctly in a similar way to the video in tip 7. If you hear an echo through your speakers during a web chat, try turning the microphone level down and asking the other person to turn their speaker volume down. If the problem persists, try wearing headphones or a headset with a microphone, as this will eliminate the feedback loop.

9 CRT WARNING

Don't attempt to fix your monitor by opening it up. This is an important safety tip. There are high voltages inside a monitor, and you could seriously injure yourself, even if the monitor has been unplugged from the mains. Whatever component might need replacing, it's almost always more cost-effective to replace the monitor with a new one. You'll probably end up with a better-quality monitor and a higher resolution in the process.

10 AVOID DATA LOSS

Eject your USB storage devices rather than just removing them. It's a pain ejecting a flash drive or memory card when you want to remove it from your PC, especially as it may seem to do no harm. However, if you pull it out before Windows has finished writing files to it (and this can happen a while after you save a document, due to Windows' delayed writes policy) you could easily lose work or corrupt files on the USB device. If Windows' eject method is too inconvenient, install a program that allows you to remove USB devices quickly, such as the free USB Disk Ejector, which you can download from *http://quick.mixnmojo.com/usb-disk-ejector*. ◻

Solving sound problems

IT'S A FAMILIAR situation: you turn your PC on and fire up your media player to listen to some music. The file appears to play, but there's no sound coming from your speakers. It's a common and frustrating problem, but is usually easy to fix.

First, check the obvious. Are your speakers switched on and the volume turned up? Are the audio cables correctly connected to your PC? If you have a laptop, does it have a mute button, or a Function key combination that allows you to mute and unmute the sound?

Next, check whether the sound is muted within Windows. You may see an icon that looks like a speaker cone in the Notification Area at the bottom of your desktop. If not, click the < button to expand the view to see all icons. Single-click on the speaker and you should see a volume slider and a Mute tickbox. Ensure that the box isn't ticked and that the volume slider isn't set to minimum. If you don't see an icon, click Start, All Programs, Control Panel. In Windows XP, click on the Sounds, Speech, and Audio Devices, then Sounds and Audio Device. In Vista's Control Panel, click Hardware and Sound, then Sound.

MULTIPLE SOUND DEVICES

Another common reason for hearing no sound is because you have multiple audio devices connected to or installed on your computer. For example, you may have recently installed a Skype handset or headset. In effect, this is a sound card in itself, and Windows can inadvertently make this the primary sound device, meaning that all sounds, whether from Windows Media Player, Internet Explorer or another application, are being routed to

the handset instead of your speakers. You can either unplug the device, which should fix the problem instantly, or you can select a different audio device in the Control Panel.

Navigate to the sound properties in the Control Panel as described above. The process differs slightly between XP and Vista. In XP, click the Audio tab and you'll see two drop-down boxes, one for Sound playback and one for Sound recording. You need to ensure the sound card to which your speakers are connected is selected. In Windows Vista, there are separate tabs for Playback and Recording, and you'll need to choose the correct device in the Playback tab.

If this doesn't solve the problem, you may need to check your sound card's audio mixer, which provides volume controls for different devices, such as the microphone, line-in and WAV. To open the mixer in XP, double-click on the speaker icon in the Notification Area. In Vista, you need to single-click the speaker icon and click the Mixer link.

DEVICE MANAGER

If you still have no joy, check that the sound card is working properly by opening Device Manager (see page 38). Scroll down the list of hardware until you come to Sound, video and game controllers. Expand the tree by clicking the + symbol, and look for any yellow exclamation marks or red crosses. Exclamation marks mean there's a problem with the hardware – drivers may not be correctly

1 Make sure the volume sliders aren't set to zero and that they're not muted

2 Surround-sound speakers such as Creative's Gigaworks G500 require multiple audio connections

3 Skype handsets can play havoc with your audio settings

4 Most sound cards have lots of identical-looking minijack inputs and outputs, so ensure you connect the cables to the right sockets

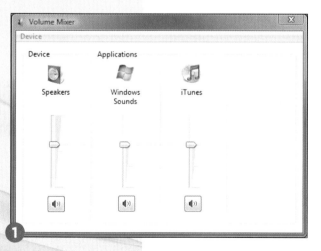

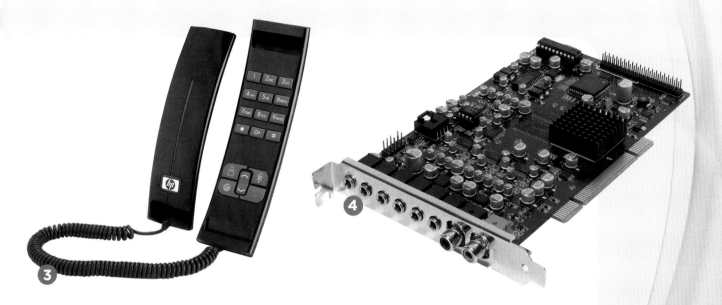

installed or the hardware itself is malfunctioning – while a red cross means the hardware is disabled.

If you see an exclamation mark next to your sound card, you'll need to reinstall the driver. This should be included on a disc that came with your computer, but if you don't have one, you'll need to download the drivers. Most PCs and all laptops have built-in sound cards, which means it's fairly easy to identify the make and model. For PCs, you can either search on the manufacturer's website or the motherboard manufacturer's site. For laptops, it's usually best to visit the manufacturer's website. You can recognise a built-in sound card by the fact that its ports are located with others on the rear of your PC, rather than on a separate card adjacent to the main ports.

If you see a red cross, you can try re-enabling the hardware by right-clicking on it and choosing Enable. You may still need to install the drivers after doing this.

CHECK THE BIOS

You may find that there are no sound devices listed in Device Manager. In this case, you should reboot your computer and enter the BIOS (for more on this, see page 102). In the BIOS, look for a menu titled Integrated peripherals, and scan the list for AC'97 or HD Audio. If it's disabled, you simply need to enable it, save the changes and exit the BIOS. When you reboot, Windows should detect new hardware and either install drivers automatically or prompt you to locate them.

If the sound card is enabled in the BIOS but doesn't show up in Device Manager, the hardware is probably faulty and you'll need a new sound card. The easiest option is to buy a USB sound card, as this won't require you to open up your PC. This is your only option if you have a laptop. If you don't mind opening your PC, you can buy a PCI sound card or, if you have a modern motherboard with PCI Express slots, a PCI-E 1x sound card.

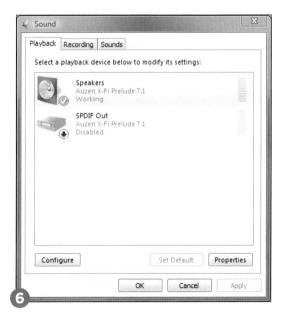

5 In Windows XP, audio devices are shown in separate lists on the same tab

6 Vista's controls show playback and recording devices on separate tabs

Solving monitor problems

AS WITH THE other peripherals covered in this chapter, monitor problems may or may not be fixable. Here we'll address a few common problems that you can solve without calling your display manufacturer.

The most obvious problem is that there's no image on the screen. You need to find out if the fault lies with your PC or your monitor. As we've already shown in Chapter 2, there are several reasons why your PC may refuse to boot, and some of them could cause the screen to be blank.

It's worth checking the basics first. Ensure that the power and signal cables are firmly attached to the monitor, as well as to the wall socket and the PC. If your monitor is plugged into a power strip, make sure that both the wall switch and any switches on the power strip are turned on.

Most monitors, whether CRT or LCD, show a warning message if no input signal is detected. If you see such a message, it's clear that the display is working. Some monitors have multiple inputs, so you need to select the appropriate one to view the incoming signal. There should be a dedicated button on the monitor for this, but it may be hidden in the onscreen menus.

If you do see a Windows screen but it's showing incorrect colours, disconnect and reconnect the video cable at both ends and tighten it securely. A loose cable is a common cause of colour corruption. If you're using a VGA cable with

an LCD screen and you see fuzzy text or the entire Windows desktop is shifted off one edge, use your monitor's Auto setting to re-sync the signal. If this doesn't work, try using the manual clock and phase options in the monitor's menu system.

Another common LCD problem is stuck pixels, where a dot constantly shows one colour (red, green, blue, white or black) irrespective of what Windows is showing. If this is the case, it's worth trying a free utility such as UDPixel from *http://udpix.free.fr* to see if it can be changed. Such applications rapidly change the colours onscreen for several hours in an effort to coax the pixel into life. UDPixel is helpful as it can show the five possible colours across the whole screen to help you identify where any defective pixels are located.

On older CRT monitors, you may see dark patches in the corners or at the edges of the screen. It's often possible to correct these by using the monitor's degauss function in the menus. If this doesn't work, move any magnetic sources such as unshielded speakers away from the monitor.

A GUIDE TO INTERFACES
VGA
VGA (also known as D-sub) has been a standard PC video connection since 1987, and is the most basic PC graphics connection. The VGA connector supports resolutions of up to 2,048x1,536. VGA connectors carry an analogue signal made up of the component colours – red, green and blue – as well as horizontal and vertical timing data.

1 Dead or stuck pixels may be fixable using a utility such as the free UDPixel

2 LCD screens can warn you if there's no signal or if a signal is out of range

3 There are several types of DVI cable

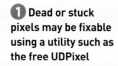

UndeadPixel 2.2

Dead pixel locator

| Red |
| Lime |
| Blue |
| White |
| Black |
| Yellow |
| Run cycle |

Press each button and locate your dead pixel.

Undead pixel

Flash windows : 1

Flash size : 5X5

Flash interval : (25 ms)

Start   Reset

Choose number and size of flashing area plus flash time interval. Then press start and move flashing area into your dead pixels.

Our website : UDPixel
Any suggestion, please send mail to : udpixel@gmail.com
Does it work ? ... so encourage people who make free software for you, make a gift : PayPal DONATE

VGA was designed for CRT monitors, which required this timing data to draw the picture using an electron gun firing in a series of lines at phosphors on the screen. LCD monitors paint the same picture using different voltages applied to rows of pixels, so they need to convert this timing data. This is done automatically and rarely causes problems, but for fine control you should look for Pixel Clock and Phase settings on your monitor's onscreen display menu. Test patterns are available on the web to help you set these up correctly.

DVI

The next step up from VGA is DVI, which supports a maximum resolution of 2,560x1,600 (the highest any consumer connection can currently offer) and can carry both analogue and digital signals. Most modern video cards have two DVI outputs. One of the most practical advantages of using a monitor with a DVI input rather than a VGA connection is that you don't need to fiddle with timing data, because in its native resolution a DVI output transmits data for each pixel on an LCD screen.

There are five main types of DVI connection (see the picture on the right), which makes it a bit more confusing than other connectors. DVI-A (Analogue) supports only analogue signals, and has the fewest pins on its connector. DVI-D (Digital) is a digital-only version found on most modern LCD monitors, and can be distinguished by the narrower flat pin, which doesn't include four pins arranged in a square around it.

DVI-I (Integrated) allows for both analogue and digital signals, and is standard on most modern video cards. DVI-I has a wider flat pin, plus the four analogue signal pins. This means that a male DVI-D connector can fit into a female DVI-I port, allowing you to connect your digital monitor to your

PC; you can also connect a DVI-to-VGA adaptor to this port or DVI-A cable, so you can plug in analogue monitors. A male DVI-I connector won't fit into the narrower flat pin on a DVI-D female port, so you can't connect incompatible devices.

To make things more confusing, there are also dual-link versions of DVI-I and DVI-D. These support higher bandwidth connections for displays over 1,920x1,200, such as huge 30in models, which can support resolutions of up to 2,560x1,600. Dual-link connectors can be distinguished by the six extra pins in the middle of the two banks of nine pins. To use dual-link, you'll also need a graphics card with a dual-link output.

HDMI

DVI has a few limitations compared to the newest standard, HDMI. As well having a standard connector to make things simpler, HDMI also carries high-definition audio and remote control signals. This means you can reduce the number of wires connected between your monitor, speakers and PC. The remote control features allow devices made by the same manufacturer to communicate with each other, so you can set timers to record TV programmes, for example.

HDMI also supports High-bandwidth Digital Content Protection (HDCP) encryption as standard. This is a copy-protection system that is standard on multimedia devices such as Blu-ray players, and you won't be able to watch copy-protected films without it. HDMI is backwards-compatible with DVI, so with the right adaptors, you can connect from a DVI port on your PC to an HDMI-equipped monitor, and vice versa. HDCP is not always enabled on DVI ports, however, so it's worth checking that both your PC and your monitor will support it.

DISPLAYPORT

The final type of connector is DisplayPort, a new digital connector that supports resolutions up to 3,840x2,160 over a single cable. This input is available on only a few current monitors, but it is becoming increasingly common on a number of graphics cards.

DisplayPort isn't compatible with HDMI or DVI, although the DisplayPort connector can pass both of these signals through. This allows graphics card manufacturers to create products that are compatible with DisplayPort and DVI monitors.

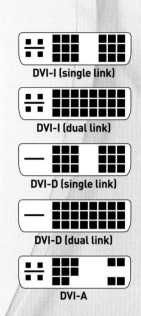

DVI-I (single link)

DVI-I (dual link)

DVI-D (single link)

DVI-D (dual link)

DVI-A

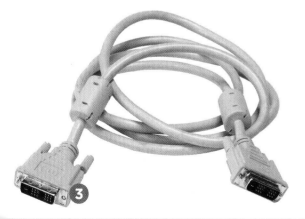

Solving printer problems

1 You can configure the default settings in your printer's driver

2 Guides in the tray should keep paper snugly in place to avoid misaligned prints

3 Prints with white lines across them could be caused by blocked nozzles

4 Laser printers may need cleaning internally from time to time

THERE ARE MANY problems you may encounter with your printer, including paper jams, misfeeds and poor print quality. Jams should be easy enough to fix without a detailed explanation here, but it's worth checking your printer's manual to find out whether there are any access hatches that let you get at paper deep inside the printer.

Misfeeds, where paper isn't picked up or isn't fed through straight, are more difficult to rectify and may require the manufacturer's assistance. Before calling a helpline, though, ensure that the paper you've inserted matches the selection in the printer driver or on the printer's front panel, as it's easy to forget you've left photo paper in the tray when you want to print on plain stock. Also ensure that any paper guides are correctly adjusted to keep paper in place as it's being fed through.

PAPER SIZE PROBLEMS
Another common problem is that print settings default to Letter paper, forcing you to change it to A4 or another metric size manually. This is easy to

correct. All you need to do is click the Printer link in Vista's Control Panel, or Printers and Faxes in XP. Find your printer in the list (there may only be one), right-click on it and choose Properties. Click Printing Preferences... at the bottom of the window. You'll see the printer's driver settings, just as you would when printing from a Windows application. However, settings you make now will become the defaults, so change the paper size and any other settings to those you want, and click OK. Finally, click OK on the printer's Properties window.

BANDING PROBLEMS
If you can see fine white lines across your prints – an effect known as 'banding' – from an inkjet printer, the cause could be blocked nozzles. There are hundreds of tiny nozzles for each colour, and they can be blocked by dust or bubbles that form inside the cartridge. The solution is either to replace the cartridge or run a cleaning cycle. There are two types of cartridges: those with integrated printheads (which contain the nozzles) and those that don't. It's easy to identify which you have, as printheads are small metal strips on the bottom of the cartridge.

Some printers allow you to print a test document, either from the controls on their front panel or via the maintenance section of their drivers. Print this and check any nozzle check patterns on the printout. From the fine grids you should be able to see how many lines are missing. If there are no patterns, there should at least be blocks of the printer's 'raw' colours, usually cyan,

magenta, yellow and black (although there may be more if you have a photo printer with extra colours). If any of these blocks have printed poorly, nozzles are blocked or the ink is running out. If a colour is completely missing, all the nozzles may be blocked (this is common if the printer hasn't been used for a long time) or the ink has run out.

It's worth getting into the habit of printing a test photograph at least once a fortnight to prevent blocked nozzles.

ALIGNMENT PROBLEMS

If you notice a mess of colours at the edges of objects in prints, the first task is to align the printheads. Many inkjet printers do this automatically when you install new cartridges, but not all have this feature. Inkjet printers work by firing miniscule dots of ink from a printhead on to the paper. If the printheads of the various colours aren't aligned, edges of objects can look fuzzy as the different coloured ink dots aren't laid down in precisely the same place.

You'll find the tool to align the printheads in your printer driver. Right-click on your printer as described in the section on paper size problems above, and choose Properties. Look for a tab called Device Settings and you'll find all your printer's settings. There will usually be a maintenance or toolbox section where you'll find an option to align the printheads. Most printers will

then print a page comprising sets of patterns in both colour and mono. Instructions onscreen may ask you to choose a pattern from each set, usually the one where the markings line up the closest. Entering this information tells the printer how to adjust itself so that it can place the tiny dots of ink from each colour in the same place.

LASER PROBLEMS

If you have a laser printer, there's not much – with the exception of paper jams – you can fix yourself when problems arise. However, if you can diagnose the problem, it may save time when calling the manufacturer's helpline.

A relatively common problem is that the toner isn't stuck fast to the paper and is easily brushed off. This indicates a fuser problem, and it's likely the fuser isn't heating up enough to melt the toner on to the page. Some fusers are user-replaceable, while others are an integral part of the printer and require the whole printer to be replaced.

Another problem is patches of toner on the page, or blank areas where toner should be. The problem could be dirt or toner on the transfer belt, drum, paper rollers or corona wires. It's inadvisable to attempt to clean the transfer belt yourself, but you can clean the rollers with a cotton swab soaked in an alcohol-based cleaner.

You can do the same with the exposed corona wires (fine wires you should find close to the paper rollers, although not all laser printers have them), but you should be much more gentle. Don't damage the wires, as this will render the printer useless. Make sure you wear latex gloves and a mask before opening up a laser printer, as you don't want to inhale any toner particles.

Chapter 5

Solving network problems

NETWORKS CAN COMPLICATE PC repairs because they introduce extra computers and hardware, all of which can go wrong. However, follow the right steps and it's fairly simple to pinpoint exactly where the problem lies. In this chapter we'll show you how to diagnose and fix all your wired and wireless networking problems. Remember to run these steps on every networked computer in order to make sure that they all work.

Network problems

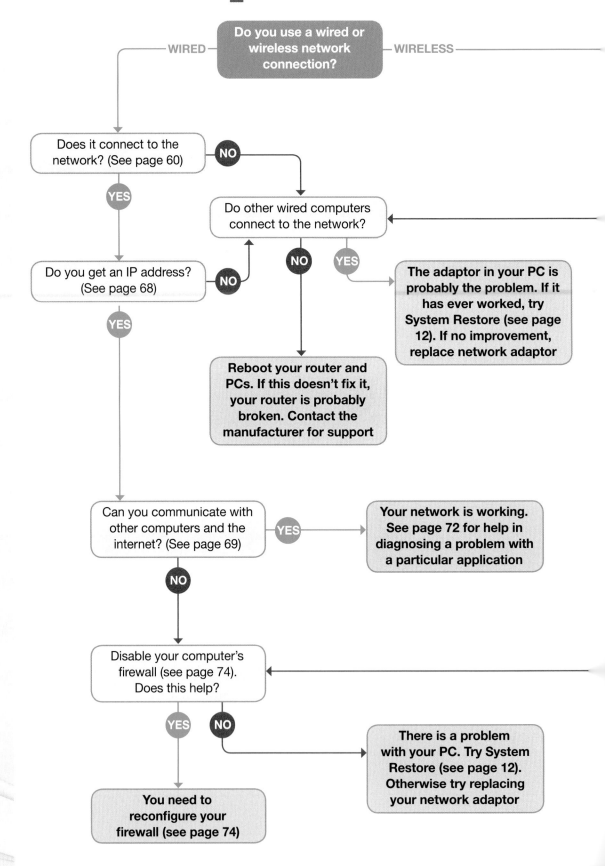

Do you use a wired or wireless network connection?

WIRED — WIRELESS —

Does it connect to the network? (See page 60)

NO

YES

Do other wired computers connect to the network?

Do you get an IP address? (See page 68)

NO

NO **YES**

The adaptor in your PC is probably the problem. If it has ever worked, try System Restore (see page 12). If no improvement, replace network adaptor

YES

Reboot your router and PCs. If this doesn't fix it, your router is probably broken. Contact the manufacturer for support

Can you communicate with other computers and the internet? (See page 69)

YES

Your network is working. See page 72 for help in diagnosing a problem with a particular application

NO

Disable your computer's firewall (see page 74). Does this help?

YES **NO**

There is a problem with your PC. Try System Restore (see page 12). Otherwise try replacing your network adaptor

You need to reconfigure your firewall (see page 74)

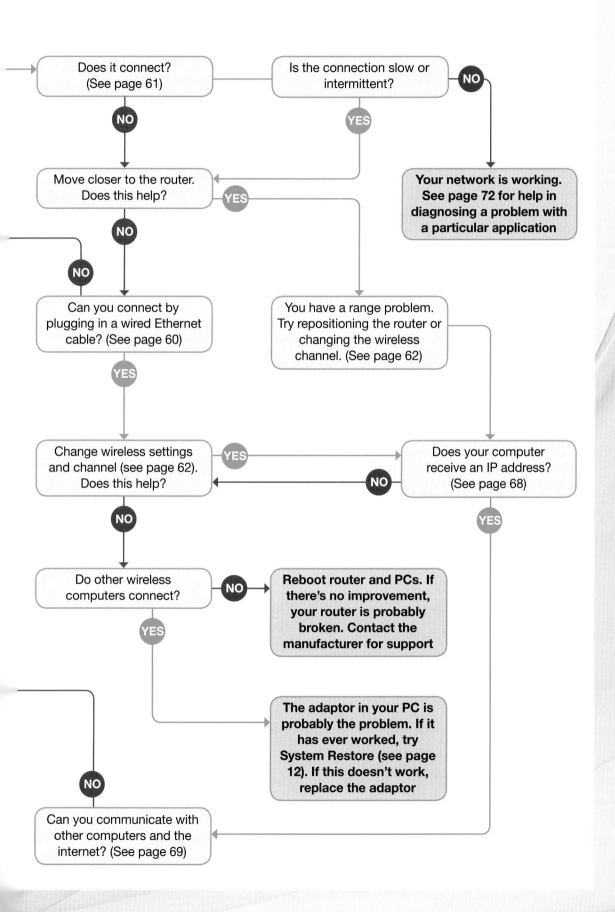

Does it connect?
(See page 61)

Is the connection slow or
intermittent?

NO

NO

YES

Move closer to the router.
Does this help?

YES

Your network is working.
See page 72 for help in
diagnosing a problem with
a particular application

NO

NO

Can you connect by
plugging in a wired Ethernet
cable? (See page 60)

You have a range problem.
Try repositioning the router or
changing the wireless
channel. (See page 62)

YES

Change wireless settings
and channel (see page 62).
Does this help?

YES

Does your computer
receive an IP address?
(See page 68)

NO

NO

YES

Do other wireless
computers connect?

NO

Reboot router and PCs. If
there's no improvement,
your router is probably
broken. Contact the
manufacturer for support

YES

The adaptor in your PC is
probably the problem. If it
has ever worked, try
System Restore (see page
12). If this doesn't work,
replace the adaptor

NO

Can you communicate with
other computers and the
internet? (See page 69)

HOW TO...
Connect a wired network

A WIRED NETWORK connection problem is easier to diagnose than a wireless connection, as there's a physical connection. Generally speaking, as long as this is plugged in correctly and there's some indication that your adaptor is working, then your network is working. First, reboot your computer and cycle the power on the router to make sure it's not a minor fault.

① CHECK STATUS LIGHT ON PC
Every network adaptor has status lights that show you whether the computer is connected to a network. Have a look at the back of your PC where the network cable is plugged in. If there's a solid green light, this indicates that your computer is correctly connected to the network. If there isn't, unplug the network cable by pressing the clip down and pulling backwards. Push the connector back into place until it clicks.

② CHECK STATUS LIGHT ON ROUTER
Just as your PC has status lights, so does your router. There are usually status lights on the front of your router for every port. Find out which port your PC is plugged into by following its cable and looking at the port number (make sure it's not plugged into the WAN port). Look for the corresponding light on the front of the router: if it's lit, you have a working connection.

③ DIAGNOSE CABLE
If your router's port isn't lit, remove the cable and plug it back in until it clicks. If there's still no light, unplug the cable and plug it back into another port. If you see a light now, you have a faulty router port. If you don't, unplug the cable from your PC and plug it into another network device in your home, then check the status lights. If you get a connection, there's a problem with your PC's network adaptor; if you don't, there's a problem with the cable and you should replace it.

④ NETWORK ADAPTOR PROBLEM
If you have a problem with your network adaptor, there are a few things that you can try. First, use Device Manager (see page 38) to find out if Windows is detecting your adaptor. If there's a problem with it, download and reinstall the driver from your motherboard manufacturer's website (see page 10). If the problem persists, you may need to buy a new network adaptor. PCI and PCI Express adaptors should cost around £10 for PCs; CardBus or ExpressCard adaptors cost around £30 for laptops. ◘

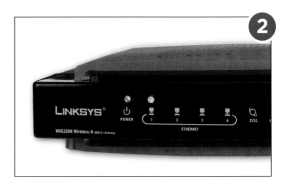

HOW TO...
Connect a wireless network

WIRELESS NETWORKS ARE slightly harder to diagnose, as sometimes you can find that your computer is connected to the network but is still not working. These instructions assume that you're using Windows' wireless network manager; if you're using software that came with your wireless adaptor, follow the manufacturer's instructions to check the settings we mention.

1 CHECK ADAPTOR IS INSTALLED
Use Device Manager (see page 38) to make sure that your wireless adaptor is detected correctly and working. If it's not in the list and it's not built into your computer, unplug it and reconnect it. If your adaptor is connected properly but showing an error message next to it, try reinstalling the drivers (see page 10). If this doesn't work, you should try replacing the adaptor.

2 CHECK CONNECTION
If your adaptor is working, check to see if it's connected to a network. In Vista, open the Control Panel and click on the View network status and tasks link. Click Connect to a network, select Wireless from the Show drop-down menu and you should see the wireless network to which you're connected at the top of the list.

In Windows XP, go to the Control Panel and click on Network and Internet Connections. Click on the Internet Connections link and double-click Wireless Network Connection. Click the View Wireless Networks button and the network to which you're connected will be at the top.

3 CHANGE WIRELESS NETWORK
If you're either not connected or you're connected to a network that isn't your own, you need to join your own network. From the wireless network list in Step 2, find your wireless network. If you can't see it, click the Refresh button in Vista (this looks like two arrows) or the Refresh network list link in XP. If you still can't see your network, there's a bigger problem and you should go back to the networking flowchart on page 58. Otherwise, double-click your network and enter the password you used when you first set up the router.

4 DELETE ALL PREVIOUS SETTINGS
If you still can't connect to your wireless network, you should delete all your previous

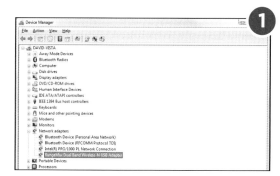

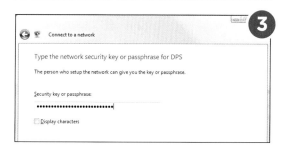

network settings. In Vista, click on the Manage wireless networks link. Select each entry in the list and click Remove. In Windows XP, click Change advanced settings and then the Wireless Networks tab. Select every entry in the Preferred networks list one at a time and click Remove. Go back to Step 3 to connect to your wireless network.

Setting up a secure wireless network

THE FOLLOWING FOUR pages will take you through configuring your wireless network securely. Before we begin, however, it's worth discussing wireless security in a little more depth and discounting some techniques that are more hassle than they're worth.

ENCRYPTING A CONNECTION
The best way to secure your wireless network is to use encryption. The original encryption standard was called Wired Equivalent Privacy (WEP). However, this standard is far from secure, so you should avoid using WEP or you risk someone breaking into your network quite easily.

A newer standard – WiFi Protected Access (WPA) – is not only more secure than WEP, it's also far easier to set up. All you have to do is use a regular password. Connecting a computer to your wireless network simply requires you to enter this same password. You therefore need to make sure that the password you choose is easy enough to remember but difficult for other people to guess. Don't use your name, house number or any other piece of information that other people could easily guess.

CHANNEL AND RANGE
In the UK, wireless networks can operate on one of 13 channels, numbered from 1 to 13. Only channels 1, 6 and 11 should be used, however, as these don't interfere with each other. If you're getting poor signal strength or an intermittent connection, switch to another channel. Draft-N wireless devices (the latest standard) operate at

their highest speeds by using two channels together in a process known as channel-bonding. If you're having problems, switch to single-channel mode (also called 20MHz or 130Mbit/s mode).

Some routers allow you to adjust the strength of the wireless signal. This can be an effective way of deterring hackers. Simply turn down the strength of your router until your house is covered, but the area outside the building isn't. This will make it harder for hackers to detect and connect to your network.

THE SERVICE SET IDENTIFIER
When you configure a wireless network, you'll need to allocate it a name. This name is also called the service set identifier, or SSID. This can be anything you want, but don't use any personal details that could identify you or your home.

Other wireless security tutorials may tell you to disable the SSID broadcast in your router. This stops your wireless router from announcing its presence, which makes it invisible to other PCs, including your own. This sounds great in practice, but it doesn't actually work very well as a serious security measure. Determined hackers can still detect your wireless network and discover its SSID. If you're using good encryption, this is as far as they will get. Hiding your SSID will deter only the most casual of snoopers.

MAC ADDRESS FILTERING
MAC address filtering is another security technique that's often touted as a good idea, but actually isn't. A MAC address is the unique hardware

1 MAC filtering is complex to set up and not very secure, so don't use it

2 Use your router's setup wizard if it has one, but check the settings using our step-by-step workshop

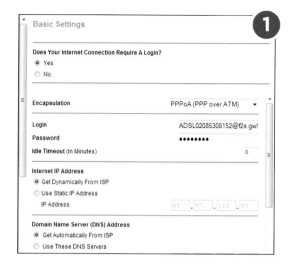

address of a computer. You can tell your router to allow only specific MAC addresses to connect to the network. While this means that you can block all but your own computers from connecting, it's difficult to manage because you have to look up the MAC addresses of your computers and enter them manually, and hackers can get round this protection easily by spoofing a valid MAC address.

HOW TO SET UP A WIRELESS NETWORK

Connect to your wireless router's web interface page using the settings in your manual. If you can't find them, run a Command prompt from the Start menu by clicking on Run and typing cmd. Type ipconfig in the terminal window that appears and note down the gateway address. Start your web browser and type http:// followed by the gateway address into the address bar. Enter your username and password.

1 CONFIGURE INTERNET SETTINGS
On the internet settings page, use the information provided by your ISP to enter your account details. This may include a username and password and, for ADSL connections, advanced options such as Encapsulation. If you can't find these details in the documentation sent when you first subscribed to your broadband service, you'll need to contact your ISP.

2 CONFIGURE WIRELESS SETTINGS
To configure your wireless network, click on the wireless settings link. Type a network name into the router. This might be labelled Name, SSID or ESSID. Use the advice above when choosing an SSID.

Next, select the wireless channel you want to use. This setting may be on a different page to the wireless name, under a link called Advanced

Wireless Settings, or something similar. Remember you can use only channels 1, 6 or 11.

3 CHOOSE DRAFT-N MODE
If you're using a Draft-N wireless router, you'll also be able to change the wireless mode from running at 300Mbit/s (or 270Mbit/s on some routers) to half this speed. However, you should do this only if you're having trouble getting a reliable connection and if changing the channel number doesn't work. Set the mode to 130Mbit/s, which will be called 20MHz mode on some routers.

4 SET ADVANCED WIRELESS SETTINGS
If you want to hide your network from casual snoopers, you can disable Allow Broadcast of Name (SSID), or any similarly named option. You may also see an option for Wireless Isolation. Turning this on prevents wireless PCs talking to other wireless PCs directly. This is useful if you're running a wireless hotspot, but for home use turning it on will just make things such as file-sharing between wireless computers impossible.

5 ENCRYPT YOUR NETWORK
Next, you need to encrypt your wireless network, the settings for which you will find in the Security section. If you have a Draft-N router, you'll probably find that you don't have a WEP option and can select only WPA-PSK or WPA2. These are the best options anyway.

If you have a choice, select the highest level of WPA security that your router supports. Next, enter a password (sometimes called a network key), following the advice we set out in the introduction.

6 TURN ON THE FIREWALL
A firewall can protect you from hackers trying to connect directly to your computer and should be ⊙

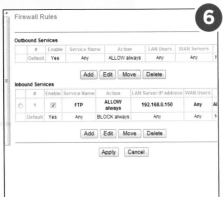

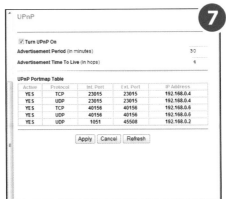

turned on. Some routers have a security section with a simple tickbox to turn the firewall on or off. Other routers, including the one we're using here, have the firewall on by default, but also allow you to create specific rules about the network traffic that's allowed through.

If you have a router such as this, you should allow all outbound but no inbound traffic unless you have a specific reason to change it. If you want to run an FTP server, for example, you'll need to allow incoming FTP traffic. If you want to prevent people on your network from using certain services, add these restrictions to the Outbound rules list.

7 TURN ON UPnP

The universal plug'n'play (UPnP) technology found on many wireless routers allows your computer to configure your router's firewall automatically to allow specific services such as video calls in Windows Live Messenger.

For the most secure environment you should turn off UPnP, but for most home networks it should be turned on simply because a lot of popular programs and services need it in order to work properly.

The option to turn on UPnP varies between routers, but there's usually either an Advanced

section of the web interface or a dedicated UPnP link you can click.

8 SET ADVANCED FEATURES

Some wireless routers let you configure advanced services such as web filtering, which can be used to help protect your children. Most routers allow you to prevent access to specific sites or filter sites using keywords, so that any URL that contains a listed word will be blocked. Be careful with this option, though; filtering by keywords such as 'sex' means harmless sites that contain the word 'Middlesex', for example, will be blocked.

9 CONFIGURE SCHEDULES

On some routers, you can create a schedule to dictate when the filtering rules should apply. To configure a schedule to do this, select the days and times you want to block certain sites and keywords, then give it a name. If you want one PC – such as yours – to be able to visit any website, you have to enter it as a trusted computer by entering its IP address. To find out what this is, run a Command prompt, type ipconfig and note down the IP address (labelled IPv4 in Windows Vista).

For the best protection, you should use a dedicated web-filtering application on any computers used by the younger members of your family. Vista has parental controls built in, and you can also buy dedicated software to do this.

⑩ SET UP REMOTE MANAGEMENT

Most routers have an option that lets you log into them remotely. When this is turned on, their web-management pages can be accessed over the internet and changed. We don't recommend that you turn this option on, as unauthorised users may try to break into your wireless router and change the settings.

If you choose to allow access to your router's management pages from over the internet, you should restrict access to computers according to their IP addresses. In the screen below, the IP address is the address of the remote internet connection, not the computer's IP address. This is an advanced setting that won't apply to most users.

⑪ TURN ON ADVANCED PROTECTION

Some routers have advanced security options to help protect your PC from internet-based attacks. The router here has an option called Disable Port Scan and DOS Protection. A port scan is where a hacker scans your network to see what services, such as FTP or web servers, are

running. From this information they can then work out the best way to attack your computers and network. A denial-of-service (DoS) attack is designed to stop a service working on your network, such as internet access.

⑫ SAVE SETTINGS AND REBOOT

Save the router's settings and let it reboot. You're now ready to connect your PC to the network. We'll assume that you're using Windows' built-in wireless network software. If additional software came with your network adaptor, its manual will show you how to use it or disable it so that you can use Windows' own software instead.

In Windows XP, double-click on the computer icon with radio waves coming out of it in the Notification Area at the bottom right of the screen. In Windows Vista, click on the icon of two computer monitors in the Notification Area and select Connect to a network. In both operating systems, select your wireless network from the list. It should have the name you gave it earlier.

Click Connect and, when prompted, type in the password you set in Step 5. If you stopped your network from broadcasting its name, you'll need to configure your network manually.

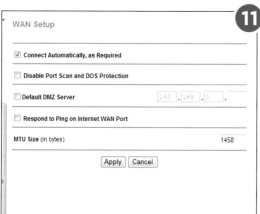

Testing your wireless network

NOW THAT YOU'VE set up your wireless network, how can you be sure that it's working securely? Fortunately, testing it isn't too hard. A number of easy-to-use free tools are available to download from the internet that can help give you confidence that your wireless network is safe from being hacked. We'll also show you some of the tools that hackers use to break into wireless networks so you'll be able see why it's so important to lock yours down properly.

You can even try out these hacking tools on your own wireless network, although some require a Linux operating system and can be fairly tricky to configure. Just knowing that they're available and what they do is enough to convince most people that proper wireless security is essential, though.

TESTING SECURITY

First, you need to make sure that you've encrypted your network properly. If you followed our tutorial on the previous page, you've already tested your network when you tried to connect to it. If you were prompted for a password when you selected your network, you know that it has been encrypted and that people can't access it without the password. You can confirm this by trying to connect from a different computer. Follow Step 12 on the previous page to do this.

GETTING A RELIABLE NETWORK

As well as having a secure wireless network, you need one that's reliable. Sometimes wireless networks can interfere with each other, causing things to slow down. If you're having trouble with yours, you can use free software to find out what other wireless networks are running in your vicinity. Go to *www.NetSumbler.com*, click Downloads and click the Download button underneath the NetStumbler heading. The MiniStumbler link is for handheld computers.

Once you've downloaded NetStumbler, install the application and run it from the Start menu. If you have the right kind of network adaptor, you should see a list of wireless networks appear in the main window. If your network adaptor isn't compatible, you'll either get an error message or nothing will happen. Most Intel network adaptors are compatible.

By expanding the Channel section in the left-hand pane, you can see which channel each network is using. This can be convenient, as you can see how many wireless networks are using the same channel as you. If, for example, your wireless network is set to channel 1 and you see that lots of other networks are also using this, you should change your wireless network to use channel 6 or 11. If there are networks on all channels, you should change yours to the least-congested one.

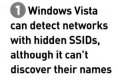

1 **Windows Vista can detect networks with hidden SSIDs, although it can't discover their names**

2 **If you see a box such as this when you connect to your network, you know that it's encrypted**

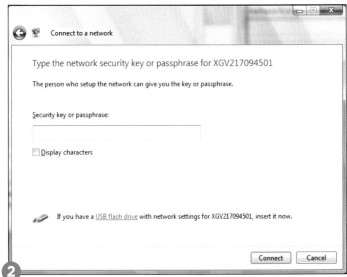

This should help you get better reception and a more reliable network.

BREAKING INTO YOUR NETWORK

Hackers have lots of tricks up their sleeves to break into wireless networks. Here we'll explain some of the techniques that they use so you can see where the weak points are and avoid the common attacks.

The easiest way for hackers to get into your network is to use a program such as NetStumbler to scan the surrounding area for wireless networks. NetStumbler provides lots of juicy information, including the name of your network (its SSID) and the make of the wireless chip inside your wireless router.

If you don't change your SSID from the one set by the manufacturer, a hacker can guess who made your wireless router. They may even be able to discover its model number. Using this information a hacker can see if there's a known security flaw with your router and exploit this to gain access to your network.

If a hacker specifically wants to break into your network, he can target you more easily if you've changed the SSID to something that identifies you, such as your house number or your name. Changing your SSID to something completely different helps mask your identity and your router's manufacturer and model number.

HIDING YOUR NETWORK

Hiding your SSID may seem a good idea, but it doesn't prevent determined hackers from attacking it. NetStumbler can still detect the network, even if its name is hidden. Windows Vista's built-in wireless software can also pick up the network, listing it as an Unnamed Network. Trying to connect to it will prompt you to type in the name of the network, but your wireless network has still been detected.

Even worse, there are some applications – such as Kismet and AirJack for Linux, AirMagnet (a commercial application for monitoring wireless networks) and AirSnort for Windows – that can uncover your SSID. These applications are relatively tricky to set up, but with constant monitoring they can find out a network's name. This is because, when a PC first connects to a wireless network, it sends the SSID in clear text.

Some of these programs even include a tool that forces a PC to disconnect from the network. When it reconnects, it will send the SSID and the hacker will be waiting to collect it. For these reasons, there's little point in hiding your SSID unless you simply want to stop casual snooping.

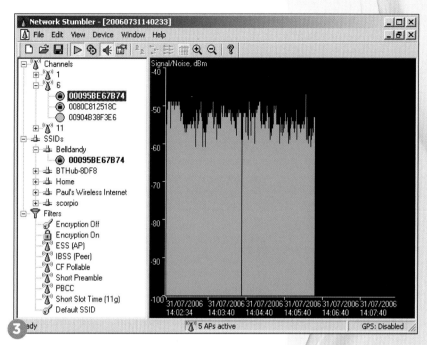

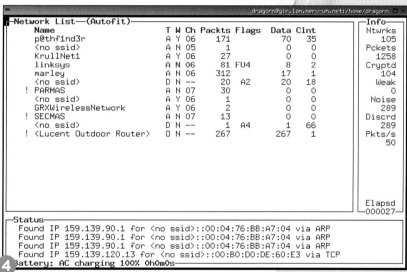

Kismet, AirJack and AirSnort can also monitor a network and use the information gathered to break the older WEP encryption keys, which effectively allowing a hacker to join your wireless network without your permission. This is why you should never use WEP encryption.

Similar tools can be used to attack WPA-protected networks, but these require more complicated attacks and rely on your password being weak. Using combinations of upper- and lower-case letters, numbers and symbols can prevent these attacks succeeding.

Although all these tools mentioned here can compromise your wireless network's security, following our advice will make it incredibly difficult for hackers to break into it. ○

③ NetStumbler can help you find out if your wireless network has any interference

④ Kismet is a Linux application that can be used to detect hidden SSIDs and break WEP keys

HOW TO...
Check your network settings

IF YOUR PC has picked up the wrong network settings, you won't be able to access the internet or other computers, even if you are connected to the network. Here we'll show you how to make sure that your computer is set up with the correct network settings and has a proper IP address, which is its unique address on the network.

① CHECK DHCP SETTINGS
The network adaptor that you use to connect to your network should be configured to use DHCP. This option lets your computer automatically receive its network settings from your wireless router. In Vista, open the Control Panel and click View network status and tasks, then click Manage Network Connections. In Windows XP, start the Control Panel and select Network and Internet Connections, then click on Network Connections.

Double-click the network connection you're using: Local Area Connection for wired networking or Wireless Network Connection for wireless. Click the Properties button. In Vista, select Internet Protocol Version 4 and click Properties. In XP, select Internet Protocol and click Properties. Make sure that Obtain an IP address automatically and Obtain DNS server address automatically are selected and click OK.

② CHECK SETTINGS
Your PC should pick up a network address automatically. To check, run Command Prompt from the Start menu. Type ipconfig and press Enter. You should see a list under the adaptor you're using that tells you the network settings of your computer. You should have an IPv4 Address (IP Address in XP) that starts 192.168.x.x; if it starts 169.x.x.x your PC hasn't received an IP address.

③ REFRESH IP ADDRESS
You can force Windows to refresh a network adaptor's IP address. Type ipconfig /release at the command prompt and press Enter, then type ipconfig /renew and press Enter. Windows should refresh your IP address settings automatically.

④ REPAIR SETTINGS
Windows can also reset the network adaptor. In Vista, go to the Network Connections dialog (see Step 1). Right-click on your network and click Diagnose. This will find and repair any problems; if none is found, click Reset the network adapter.

In Windows XP, go to the Network Connections dialog (see Step 1). Right-click the network that you're using and click Repair. This will reset your network adaptor. ⊙

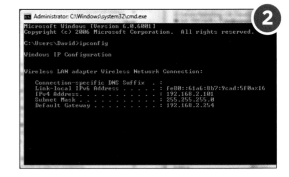

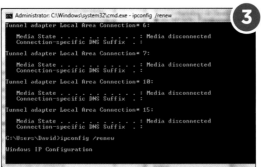

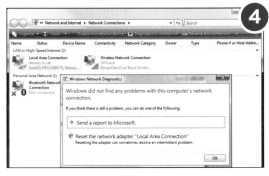

HOW TO...
Check for other computers

WHEN YOU'VE CHECKED that you're connected to a network, you should check that you can see the computer that you want to talk to. Windows has built-in tools to do this. The most useful one is Ping, which simply lets you see if a remote computer will respond to your request. Here we'll show you how to use this simple command.

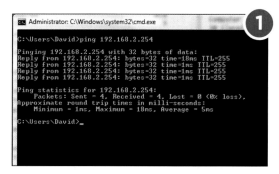

1 CHECK YOU CAN SEE YOUR ROUTER

The first step is to make sure that you can communicate with your wireless router. Start a command prompt from the Start menu and type ipconfig, make a note of the Default Gateway address that's listed. It should be something like 192.168.x.x. Type ping <default gateway address>. If you get four Reply messages, it means that you've successfully connected to your router and your PC can see it.

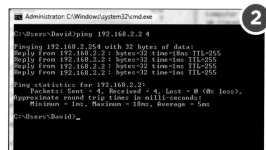

2 CHECK YOU CAN COMMUNICATE WITH ANOTHER PC

You can use the ping command to find out if you can communicate with another PC. To do this, you need to find out the other computer's IP address. From a command prompt on the other computer, type ipconfig. Make a note of its IP address.

On the original computer, type ping <other computer's IP address>. If you get four Reply messages, it means that you can communicate with that computer.

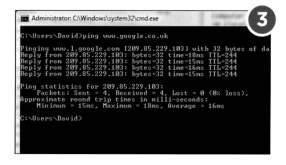

3 CHECK COMMUNICATION WITH THE INTERNET

You can also use the ping command to see if you can communicate with a web server on the internet. Some web servers are configured not to respond to ping requests, so you can only use this step on some servers. Google accepts ping requests, so it's a good one to use.

Type 'ping www.google.com'. If you get four replies, your computer is connected to the internet properly. If you don't, there's a problem, and your router's not connected to the internet.

4 MAKE SURE DNS IS WORKING

You can verify if you have a connection to the internet by using another command that tests the Domain Name Service (DNS). This is the internet technology that converts the easy-to-remember web addresses that we use into IP addresses that

computers use. If you're not connected to the internet, this service won't work and your web browser will be unable to connect to any websites.

Type 'nslookup www.google.com'. You should get a result that gives you a set of IP addresses listed under 'Addresses:'. If you get an error message, it means that you're not connected to the internet properly.

Chapter 6

Solving internet problems

IF YOU'RE STILL having trouble with your computers once you know that your network is working and that your PC can communicate with other computers and the internet (see page 69), you can narrow the problem down to one of two things: software or your ISP. In this chapter, we'll take you through the steps to detect and solve these problems.

Internet and network application problems

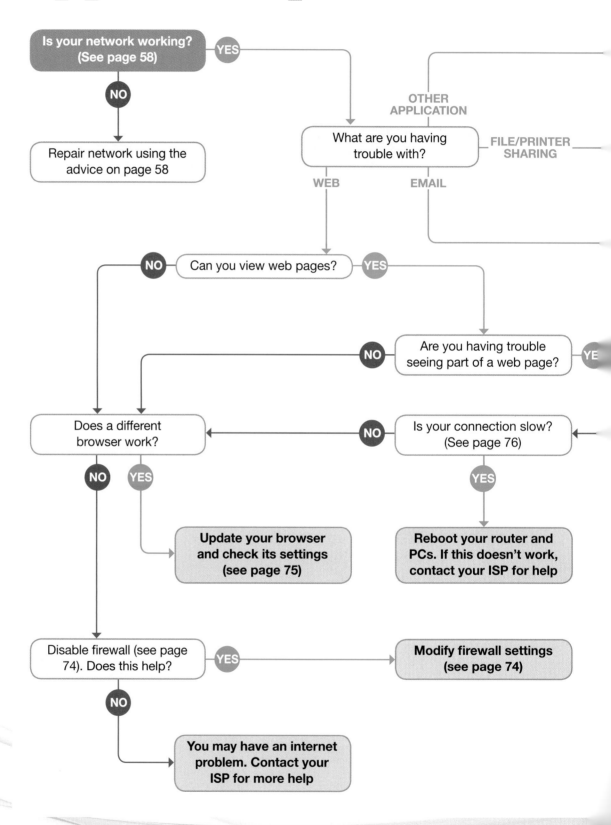

Is your network working?
(See page 58) — YES

NO

Repair network using the advice on page 58

OTHER APPLICATION

What are you having trouble with?

FILE/PRINTER SHARING

WEB   EMAIL

NO — Can you view web pages? — YES

NO — Are you having trouble seeing part of a web page? — YE

Does a different browser work? — NO — Is your connection slow? (See page 76)

NO   YES

Update your browser and check its settings (see page 75)

YES

Reboot your router and PCs. If this doesn't work, contact your ISP for help

Disable firewall (see page 74). Does this help? — YES — **Modify firewall settings (see page 74)**

NO

You may have an internet problem. Contact your ISP for more help

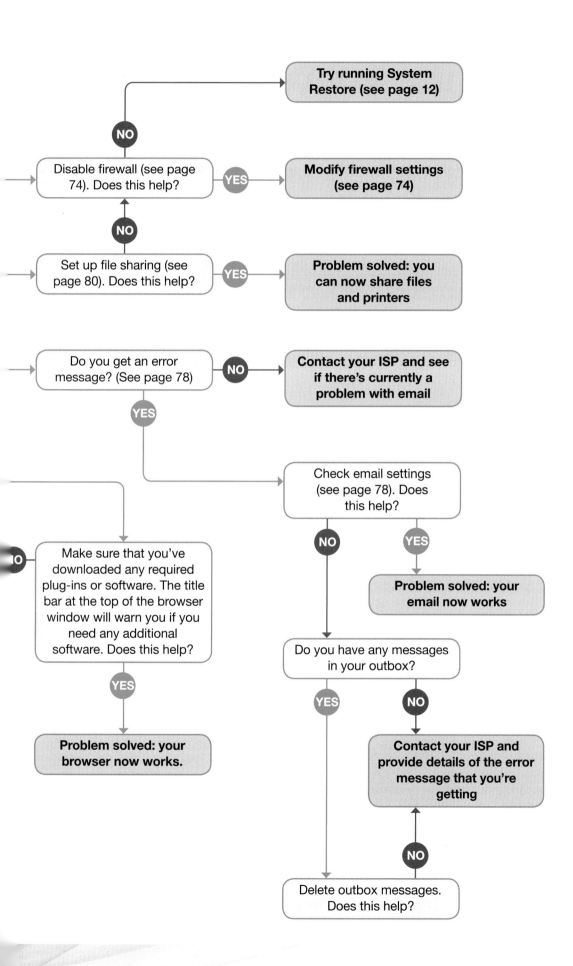

Try running System Restore (see page 12)

NO

Disable firewall (see page 74). Does this help?

YES → **Modify firewall settings (see page 74)**

NO

Set up file sharing (see page 80). Does this help?

YES → **Problem solved: you can now share files and printers**

Do you get an error message? (See page 78)

NO → **Contact your ISP and see if there's currently a problem with email**

YES

Check email settings (see page 78). Does this help?

NO   **YES**

Problem solved: your email now works

Make sure that you've downloaded any required plug-ins or software. The title bar at the top of the browser window will warn you if you need any additional software. Does this help?

YES

Problem solved: your browser now works.

Do you have any messages in your outbox?

YES   **NO**

Contact your ISP and provide details of the error message that you're getting

NO

Delete outbox messages. Does this help?

HOW TO...
Configure your firewall

WINDOWS FIREWALL

Your PC is protected by a software firewall, which can stop some internet applications from working. Here we'll show you how to configure your firewall. We're using the Windows Firewall, but the steps will be similar if your security software has a built-in

firewall – read its manual for full information. To start Windows Firewall Settings in XP, go to the Control Panel, click Windows Security Center and click Windows Firewall. In Vista, go to the Control Panel and click 'Allow a program through Windows Firewall'.

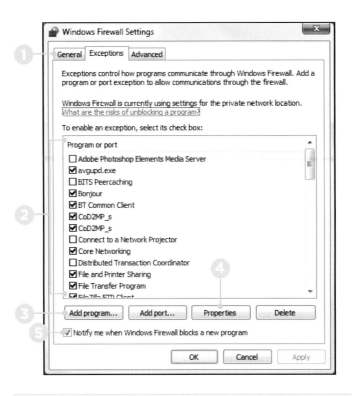

1 GENERAL TAB This lets you disable or enable the firewall.

2 PROGRAMS Put a tick in the box next to a program's name to allow it access through the firewall.

3 ADD PROGRAM You can add any program not listed here.

4 PROPERTIES Select a program and click Properties for more information about it.

5 NOTIFY ME Make sure that this is selected so that you'll be warned if the Firewall is blocking an application.

Your router's firewall needs to be configured properly for your internet connection to work correctly

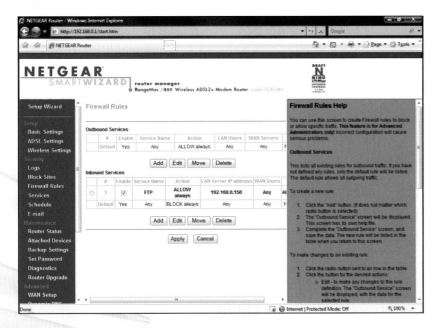

ROUTER FIREWALL

Your wireless router also has a built-in firewall that protects all your computers from internet threats. To change its settings, connect to the router's web-based management page by running Command Prompt from the Start menu, typing ipconfig and making a note of the Gateway Address. Type this address into your web browser's address bar and you'll be prompted to log on to the router's management page.

Some applications, such as games, require you to configure networking ports for the application to work. You can get more information about this at *www.portforward.com*. You should also turn on UPnP, if your router supports it, as this lets your computers automatically configure the router's firewall on demand. Your router's manual will give you full instructions on this, as do our instructions on configuring a wireless network on page 62.

HOW TO...
Check your browser settings

IF YOU'RE HAVING internet problems, it makes sense to check your browser settings and update to the latest version. We've included the instructions for Internet Explorer (IE) and Firefox here, but other browsers are similar. To get the latest versions, go to *http://tinyurl.com/ieupdate* for IE, *www.firefox.com* for Firefox and *www.google.co.uk/chrome* for Google Chrome.

Internet Explorer

Go to File, Options to see these settings.

1 PRIVACY The option in this tab should be set to Medium, or some websites won't work correctly

2 CONNECTIONS This tab gives you access to the settings information that you see here.

3 DIAL-UP SETTINGS If you connect via a modem, your settings should be here. If you use a wireless router, remove every entry here.

4 LAN SETTINGS This lets you configure your network settings if you use a wireless router (see numbers 5 and 6 below).

5 AUTOMATIC CONFIGURATION Unless specified by your ISP, you should leave these tick boxes blank.

6 PROXY SERVER Unless specified by your ISP, you shouldn't need this.

Firefox

1 NETWORK This tab configures how your browser connects to the internet.

2 SETTINGS Click this button to configure the connection options (see 3 and 4 below).

3 CONFIGURE PROXIES Unless specified by your ISP, you shouldn't need this.

4 AUTOMATIC PROXY CONFIGURATION Unless specified by your ISP, this should be left blank

HOW TO...

Speed-test your broadband connection

TESTING THE SPEED of your broadband connection can help you track down internet problems. To do this, go to *www.speedtest.net* and follow the instructions below.

You should compare the results that you get from this test with the quoted speed of your internet connection. Anything wildly below the quoted speed indicates that you may have a problem with your internet connection. Before you contact your ISP, try running the test from another PC in the house; a fast connection here means that the problem is with the first computer you tested.

① SET UP YOUR PC FOR TESTING

Before you start, it's important to iron out any problems that may slow down your test. A slow wireless network could make it look as though your broadband is running slower than it actually is. For that reason, it's best to test your connection from a PC that's plugged directly into the router via a cable. If it's not close to hand, then move your PC or laptop to the router, if possible, and plug it in. If you can't do this, then move your wireless PC or laptop as close to the router as you can get so that you get the strongest signal and best speeds.

No matter what connection you're using, make sure that nobody in your house is using the internet, particularly for downloading large files. If they are, this will skew your results and make your broadband connection look slower than it is.

② CHECK THE TEST SERVER

Open your web browser and visit *www. speedtest.net*. You'll be taken to the SpeedTest.net website, which should zoom into a map of where you live, highlighting a star in gold. This indicates the recommended server that you should use to test your connection. It works this information out by using your computer's Internet Protocol (IP) address, which is its unique address on the internet. This tells SpeedTest.net which ISP you're using and, therefore, where you're located.

UK users should have a gold star in the UK highlighted. If this is the case, click on Test Using Recommended Server at the top of the map, and skip to Step 4.

③ MANUALLY SELECT A SERVER

If SpeedTest.net failed to identify which server you should be using, you'll have to do the job manually. However, this isn't difficult.

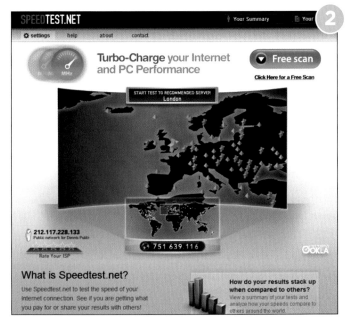

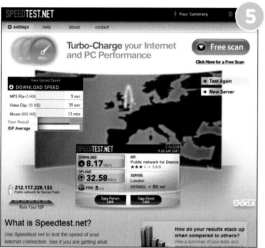

Hover your mouse over the gold star and select London from the list.

4 RUN THE TESTS

SpeedTest.net now tests your connection in a number of different ways. First, it will test your connection's ping speed. This is how quick your connection is to respond; the faster the time here, the better it is for playing games.

Next, an automated download test takes place. This downloads a file from the test server and times how long it takes. Finally, an upload test takes place. This times how long it takes to send a file to the server in question. When the test has finished, you'll automatically be redirected to the results page.

5 CHECK YOUR RESULTS

Your speed test results are displayed in the main window. The most important statistics are located in the middle of the screen. The download speed is the figure that tells you how fast your internet connection is. This is also the figure that

you should compare to the broadband speed that you're paying for. SpeedTest.net presents this figure in megabits per second (it denotes this as Mb/s).

If this figure is the same as or very close to the service you're paying for, you don't have a problem with your connection; if it's significantly slower, there could be a problem with your ISP, or it may be because you live a long way from your ADSL exchange. Try rebooting your router and testing again. If there's no improvement, contact your ISP.

6 COMPARE RESULTS

Once you have your results, you can click Test Again to try the speed test again. It may be worth trying at a different time of day, as the connection may be slower at peak times during the day. You can also browse other results by clicking Your Summary. This will bring up a list of your previous tests, while clicking on World Summary will let you compare your broadband speed to other people's results and find out how good – or bad – your connection really is.

HOW TO...
Check your email settings

MORE OFTEN THAN not, a problem with email is usually caused by your ISP having problems. Still, there's no harm in checking other possibilities. Here we'll show you how to check that your email is configured properly and how to detect other problems. First contact your ISP and ask for the email server settings, so that you can compare your email client's settings.

We've used Windows Mail, but every email client has similar settings. Select Accounts from the Tools menu. Then select the email account you're having trouble with and click Properties.

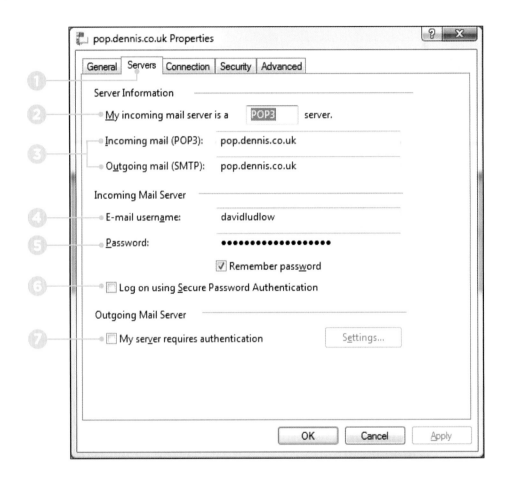

SERVERS Select this tab to get the full configuration settings.

INCOMING MAIL SERVER Make sure that this is the correct type of server. There's a choice between IMAP and POP3 for ISP email. If you have the wrong setting, you'll need to delete your account and create a new one.

INCOMING AND OUTGOING MAIL Make sure that you have the correct servers set up or you'll be unable to send or receive email.

USERNAME This needs to be entered exactly as your ISP gave it to you.

PASSWORD Make sure this is set correctly.

PASSWORD AUTHENTICATION Tick this box only if your ISP tells you to.

OUTGOING MAIL SERVER This option is usually required only if you're using email other than your ISP's, or you're using your ISP's email on a different network, such as at a wireless hotspot.

HOW TO...
Diagnose error messages

IF YOU HAVE an email problem, your email client will usually display a box giving you some information about what went wrong. Here we'll show you how to diagnose what these error messages mean, using three of the most common messages. It's also worth typing any error codes into Google, as you'll find out more information on the problem and possibly even a solution.

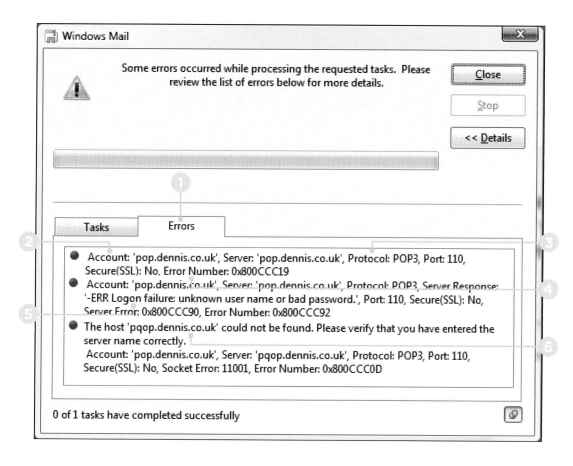

ERRORS Click this tab to see the detailed error messages.

ACCOUNT This tells you which email account has had the problem.

PROTOCOL POP3 and IMAP are problems with incoming mail; SMTP is outgoing mail.

ERROR NUMBER 0x800CCC19 This particular error message indicates a timeout problem, which could be caused by anti-virus software or your ISP's mail servers being slow to respond. It's worth entering the error code into Google to find out more.

ERROR LOGON FAILURE Look for text-based error messages: this one tells us that the wrong username or password have been entered. Check your settings using the information on the opposite page. If they're correct, contact your ISP and tell them there's a problem.

ERROR HOST COULD NOT BE FOUND This tells you that there's problem contacting the named email server. It could be that you've entered the wrong information (here we've typed pqop.dennis.co.uk instead of pop.dennis.co.uk), or it could mean that your ISP's email servers have stopped working. If this is the case, contact your ISP for more details.

HOW TO...
Share files and printers

ONE OF THE main benefits of having a network is that you can share files and printers between all the computers on your network. Here we'll show you how to set this up in Vista and XP.

① VISTA FILE AND PRINT SHARING

Open the Control Panel and select Network and Internet, then Set up file sharing. Under Sharing and Discovery, expand Network discovery, click Turn on network discovery and click Apply. Expand File sharing, click Turn on file sharing and click Apply.

If you have a printer installed on your computer and want to share it, expand Printer sharing, click Turn on printer sharing and click Apply.

② VISTA SECURITY

By default Windows Vista requires you to give everyone that you want to share files with a username and password, which you create through the Control Panel's Users application. When you share a folder or printer you then select which users you want to have access. This can get a bit complicated, so it's usually best to turn password-protected access off. Expand the Password protected sharing section, click Turn off password protected sharing and click Apply.

③ SHARE A VISTA FOLDER

To share a folder and files in Windows Vista, use Windows Explorer to navigate to the folder that you want to share. Right-click it and select Share. Select Everyone from the drop-down list and click Add. Next to Everyone in the main window, change the permission level: Reader lets network users read files only, Contributor lets them create, modify and delete their own files, and Co-owner lets them create, modify and delete all files.

④ SHARE AN XP FOLDER

Sharing in Windows XP is easier to set up. Navigate to the folder you want to share in Windows XP, right-click it and select Sharing and Security. Click the 'If you understand the security risks but want to share files without running the wizard, click here' link. In the dialog box that appears, select Just enable file sharing. Select Share this folder on the network. If you want users to be able to delete and create files as well, tick Allow network users to change my files. Click OK.

⑤ SHARE A PRINTER

Sharing a printer is similar in Windows XP and Vista. In Vista, open the Control Panel and click on the Printers link under Hardware. In

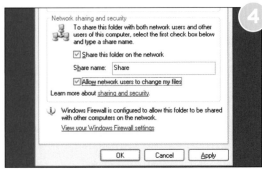

Windows XP, open the Control Panel and click Printers and Other Hardware, then click View installed printers or fax printers. In both operating systems, right-click the printer that you want to share, click Sharing, put a tick in the Share this printer box and click OK.

6 CONNECT TO A COMPUTER

To access a shared folder on the network, you can use the network browser to discover a computer. In Vista, select Network from the Start menu. In XP, select My Network Places from the Start menu, then click View workgroup computers. Simply double-click on the computer to which you want to connect. If you can't find any computers, you can connect to another computer directly.

To do this, run Command Prompt from the Start menu on the PC you want to connect to and type ipconfig. Note down the computer's IP address. On the PC you want to connect from, click Run on the Start menu and type \\<*the ip address you noted down*>. This will enable your PC to connect directly to the other computer.

If this doesn't work and you get an error message, either your PC or the remote computer is not properly connected to the network (see page 58) or there's a firewall problem (see page 74).

7 ACCESS PRINTERS AND FOLDERS

Once you connect to the remote PC, you'll see a list of shared folders and printers. Double-click on a folder to access it and its files. You can now use this folder in the same way that you'd use a folder on your computer.

Double-click on a printer to install it on your computer. You can now print documents using this printer as you would on a printer connected directly to your PC. As long as the remote computer is turned on, this printer will be available, even after you restart Windows.

8 MAP A NETWORK DRIVE

Rather than having to navigate to a network computer every time that you want to share files, you can map a network drive. This puts a normal drive letter in Computer (My Computer in XP) that you can access in the same way as a normal hard disk. Right-click on the folder to which you want to map a drive letter and select Map network drive. Choose a drive letter from the drop-down menu (letters towards the end of the alphabet are best to avoid conflict with physical drives) and click Finish.

The drive letter you select will be available every time you start Windows provided that the remote computer is turned on.

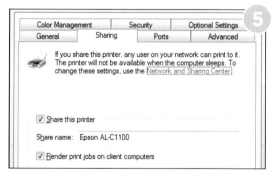

Chapter 7

Preventing problems

PREVENTION REALLY IS better than a cure when it comes to computers. In this chapter we'll show you how to spring-clean your PC, make a backup of all of your files and operating system, install an anti-virus package and tune your computer so that it runs smoothly.

Follow the advice here and you're sure to run into fewer problems in the future and bounce back more quickly from those you do encounter.

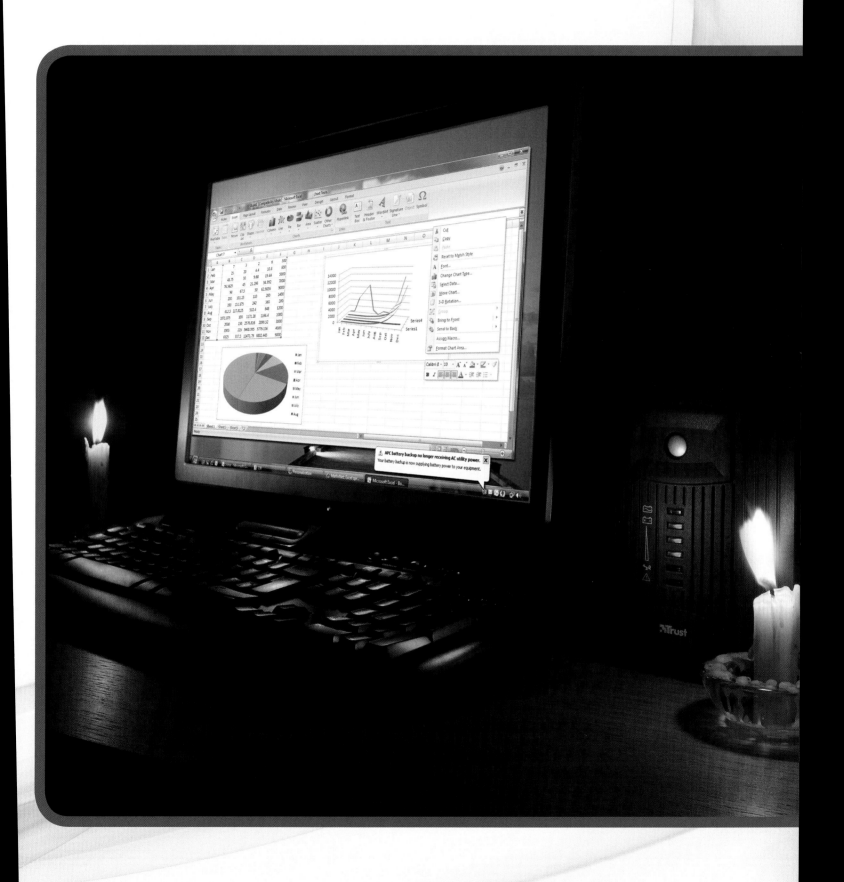

Making an image of your hard disk

GETTING YOUR PC set up exactly the way you want it is a time-consuming job. From configuring your desktop so that it suits your personal preferences to installing all your favourite applications, it can be hours of work. Add to that the fact that your PC is home to all your precious photos, videos and documents, and your computer's not just something you've spent a lot of time on, it's a record of your life.

Imagine how you'd feel if your PC suddenly shut down, taking your hard disk with it. Thankfully, this is very unlikely, but a more probable scenario is that as time goes on Windows will become increasingly bloated. Over the years, you will install and uninstall any number of extra applications and additional hardware, all of which will leave a large number of extra files and services on your hard disk. These will slow your PC down to a crawl, and reinstalling everything from scratch isn't a huge amount of fun – and you may end up losing some important files.

This is where using a disk-imaging program can save you a world of trouble. It will take a complete copy of your hard disk, including the operating system, your applications, all your settings and every file on your hard disk.

① To recover from a system error quickly, you need an image of your hard disk

NO MORE REINSTALLING
When restored, the image will take your computer back to the day that the image was made. Instead of having to reinstall Windows when it's no longer working the way you want it, you can just flash the image back and return to when you first installed Windows, complete with all your original settings and applications. So instead of hours of work, with a disk-imaging application it takes only a fraction of the time.

The best thing is that you're not just limited to taking one image. With the right software, you can also schedule images to occur regularly, so that you're constantly making a backup. If you should suffer a problem, you simply restore your computer back to the last good image – a little like a super System Restore.

Disk-imaging applications also include standard file backup options, so you can take fewer regular images, which use a lot of disk space, but still protect all your data.

HARD DISK
Ideally, you should store images on an external hard drive so you won't lose them if your main hard disk fails. This also means that you can restore the image to your old hard disk (or to a new one in the case of a major problem), getting up and running again in a short period of time. You could also back up to a secondary partition on your primary hard disk.

NORTON GHOST
We can't stress the importance of using disk-imaging software enough, particularly if you don't have a recovery disc. Most new computers come with a recovery disc, but if yours didn't – or you've mislaid it – you can make your own.

Over the next few pages, we'll show you how to make an image of your PC using the best application on the market: Norton Ghost 14. We used the download version of Ghost, which costs £40 and is available from *www.symantec.co.uk* (click on the online store). This is identical to the boxed version, although the installation steps may differ very slightly. You'll also have to download the recovery CD image file, which we'll show you how to use later.

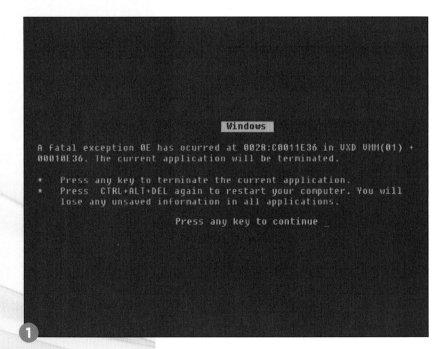

HOW TO...
Make a hard disk image

① INSTALL GHOST
Run the Ghost installation program and follow the wizard. The software should install quickly and automatically, without asking you any questions. When it's finished, you'll be prompted to restart your computer. Do this and wait for your PC to load Windows again. When prompted, enter the product key that you were provided with when you bought the application, click Next, and then click Next again to run LiveUpdate and to download the latest version of the software. Restart your computer again if prompted.

② CHANGE SCHEDULE
After LiveUpdate has finished, the Easy Setup application starts. This automatically sets up a scheduled imaging job and a scheduled file backup job. These tend to be a bit extreme, though, so you should change some settings.

First, under My Computer Backup, click the box next to Schedule to specify when you want a backup taken. The default is set for every Sunday and Thursday, but once a week should be enough. These backups record only the changes made since the last image, which saves on disk space.

Ghost is also set to create a full new image set, which takes up a lot of disk space, once every three months. This should be fine for most people.

③ ADD TRIGGERS
You can also set Ghost to run a backup when certain triggers are detected. Click on the General link under Event Triggers, and select the options you want – when any application is installed, for example. Be warned that using any of these options will increase the amount of disk space you'll need for backups, so use them carefully. When you're happy with your settings, click OK.

④ MANAGE FILES
Ghost will also take regular file backups. It's set by default to back up the Documents, My Video, My Pictures and My Music folders, Internet Explorer favourites and desktop settings. Click on the blue text to the right of Select at the top of the screen to add more options. Click OK when you're done. You can now change the schedule for this backup in the same way as in Step 3.

Finally, Norton Ghost tries to pick a suitable backup destination, such as an external hard disk. ◗

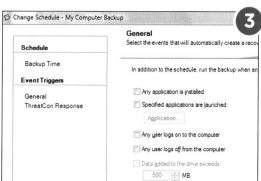

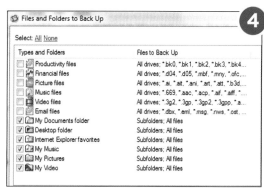

> **💡 TIP**
> A second physical hard disk or external disk are the best places for backups, as they won't be affected if your main hard disk fails.

You can also back up to a separate partition, if you've created one. This will be safe from Windows crashes, but not hard disk faults, so an external hard disk is the safest option. Use the secondary partition if you don't have an external disk. Click OK, select Run first backup now and click OK again.

5 MANAGE BACKUPS

While your backups will run to the schedule you set, you can modify this or choose to start a backup manually if, for example, you've just saved a lot of new files or made a major system change.

Start Norton Ghost and select Run or Manage Backups. The next window will display your current jobs. Select one and click Run Now to run it. You can change schedules and edit what's being backed up by clicking Edit Settings. You can now add your own custom files and folders to the default My Documents Backup.

6 RECOVER FILES

If you want to recover individual files, click Recover My Files from Ghost's main screen. You can search for a specific file or click Search to find all your backed-up files. Right-clicking a file or folder lets you view the different backup versions and recover the one you want. You can also restore files from an image. Click Recovery Point, select

the backup you want and choose Explore from Tasks. You can browse the image like a regular folder and drag files to your computer.

7 RECOVER A HARD DISK

You can restore an image to a hard disk by selecting the Recover My Computer link from Ghost's Welcome page. Select the recovery point you want and click Recover now. Provided the recovery point isn't for your boot partition (the one with Windows on it), Ghost will restore the image. If it is for your boot hard disk, Ghost can't recover it while Windows is running. Instead, you need to follow Steps 8 to 12 to create a recovery CD.

8 CREATE A RECOVERY CD

If you bought the download version of Ghost, you should have also downloaded the recovery CD image file. This needs to be burnt to a CD. You can do this with CD-writing software such as CDBurnerXP (*http://cdburnerxp.se*). If you don't have CDBurnerXP, you can download ISO Recorder from *http://isorecorder.alexfeinman.com*. Version 2 is for Windows XP and version 3 is for Vista, so make sure that you get the right one. Install the software.

Browse to the directory to which you downloaded Norton Ghost and look for the Zip file (NGH140_AllWin_EnlishEMEA_SrdOnly.zip). Open

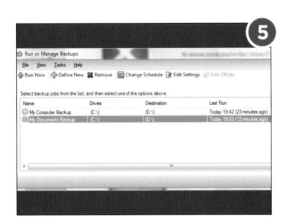

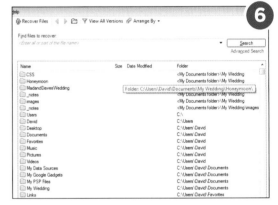

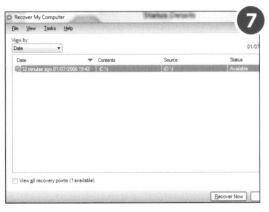

this by right-clicking on it and selecting Extract. Right-click on the resulting ISO file and select Copy image to CD. Click Next and then Finish when the operation is done. You now have a bootable restore CD.

⑨ BOOT FROM YOUR RESTORE DISC

Make sure that your BIOS is set to boot from your optical drive (see page 104) and then restart your PC. You'll be prompted to hit a key to boot off the CD, so make sure you're ready. When the Windows loading screen starts, click Accept to agree to the Norton Ghost licence agreement.

There are several options on the next screen. Click on Analyze to perform system tests, and Check Hard Disk for Errors to run a system scan on your hard disk. The Virus scanner is useful only if you've also got Symantec Anti-Virus; otherwise the definitions will be too old. You can also click on Explore your hard disk.

⑩ ADD DRIVERS

While this recovery disc will recognise most hard disks, it can't identify them all, particularly if you're running RAID. If the image you want to restore is saved on a networked hard disk, then you may have to install a driver for the network adaptor, too. To do this, click on Utilities and then Load drivers. You need to use the Explorer-like window to navigate to a folder with the relevant driver in it. You can plug in USB drives or use a CD, so adding extra drivers shouldn't be hard. You should also have them available if you had to add extra drivers when installing Windows.

⑪ RECOVER YOUR COMPUTER

Click on Home and Recover my Computer. Select the recovery point you want to restore (if the list is blank, select View by filename and click Browse to find it) and click Next. Click Finish and then Yes to start recovering your PC. The files will then be restored to your computer.

Once this has finished, you can reboot your computer and it will be back to the exact state at which you made the recovery point.

⑫ RECOVER FILES

Alternatively, you can use this interface to recover individual files from a restore point. Select Recover from the main screen and then Recover My Files. Navigate to a recovery point, select it and click OK. You'll then be presented with the Symantec Recovery Point Browser.

You can navigate through this like an ordinary disk. When you find the file or files that you want to recover, you just have to select them and click Recover Files. You can then choose where to restore the files to, such as another disk or drive. ⬤

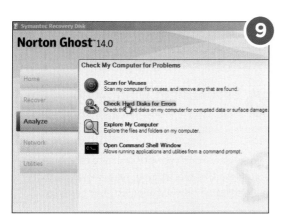

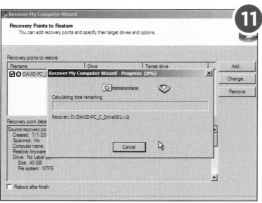

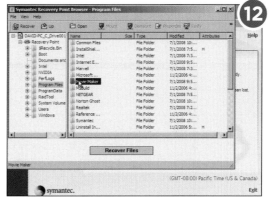

ⓞ TIP
You should run a hard disk scan (see page 88 for details of how to do this) before recovering your files to make sure there's nothing wrong with your disk.

HOW TO...
Maintain your hard disk

BY REGULARLY CHECKING your hard disk using the tools built into Windows, you can help maintain your computer and avoid potential problems. Here we'll show you how to use Check Disk and Disk Degfragmenter. Check Disk scans your hard disk for errors and can fix some serious problems, while Disk Defragmenter improves performance by reassembling files that have been split into smaller chunks and spread over the disk surface.

① ACCESS DISK TOOLS
Open Computer from the Start menu (My Computer in XP). Right-click on the disk you want to manage, such as C:, and select Properties. Click on the Tools tab to view the available options.

② CHECK FOR ERRORS
Click Check Now to start the Check Disk application, which will scan your hard disk for errors and fix problems. Click Automatically fix file system errors to repair the disk. If you want to scan the surface of your hard disk, click Scan for and attempt recovery of bad sectors. Only use this option if you've had warning messages when you turn on your PC, or you've had lots of errors in Windows saying that a file can't be read.

Click Start and, if you get a dialog box asking you to schedule a scan, click Schedule disk check (Yes in Windows XP). You'll get this dialog box if you want to scan the hard disk from which you boot Windows. You'll need to restart your

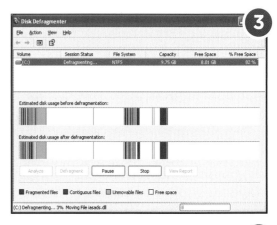

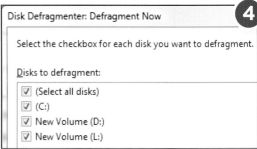

computer to complete this check. If you didn't get a message, Windows will carry out the check on the hard disk straight away.

③ DEFRAGMENT WINDOWS XP
Right-click the disk you want to defragment and click Properties. Click the Tools tab and select Defragment Now. Click the Defragment button and Windows will analyse your disk and reorganise your files. This process can take a few hours, depending on how fragmented your hard disk is.

④ DEFRAGMENT WINDOWS VISTA
Right-click the disk that you want to defragment and click Properties. Click the Tools tab and select Defragment Now. Your hard disk should be scheduled to be defragmented once a week, so your computer should already be optimised. If Disk Defragmenter is not scheduled, click Run on a schedule. To defragment a hard disk now, click Defragment now, select the hard disks you want to clean up and click OK. Windows will display a message telling you that your hard disks are being defragmented. This process can take a few hours to complete. ◻

HOW TO...
Use Windows Update

WINDOWS UPDATE WILL keep your PC running at its best and is essential for new Windows installations. Here's how to use it.

❶ GET THE UPDATER
For complete control over what you install on your PC, it's better to use Windows Update manually. Using Internet Explorer, go to *www.windowsupdate.com* (in Vista, select Windows Update from the Start menu). A security warning will ask if you want to install the Windows Update software. Click the Install button. A page opens and asks you to get the latest Windows Update software. Click Install Now, then wait a few minutes as it installs.

❷ GET UPDATES
Once the software is installed, you'll see a welcome screen with two buttons: Express and Custom (Install updates and View available updates in Vista). If you click Express, it will install the major updates. We recommend clicking Custom instead. This allows you to choose exactly which updates you install. You'll see a message saying that the website is checking for the latest updates. In XP and earlier, a screen asks you to

upgrade some components of the Windows Update software. Click Download and Install Now. A window appears with a blue progress bar. Once it's finished, click Restart when prompted.

❸ CUSTOMISE YOUR UPDATES
Using Internet Explorer, reconnect to *www.windowsupdate.com*. You'll skip to the welcome screen. Click Custom as before. After a few seconds, you'll see a page called Customise your Results. It shows a list of all the high-priority updates available. Browse through and untick any that you don't want. You can also browse updates for your other Microsoft software and for hardware drivers by clicking the Software, optional and Hardware, optional links on the left (these are displayed in the main list in Vista).

❹ INSTALL UPDATES
Once you've selected everything you want, click Install Updates at the top left (Install in Vista). You're told the number of updates and an estimated download time. If you're happy, click Install Updates. Accept the licence agreement. The updates download and install in turn. When the updates have all finished, click Restart Now.

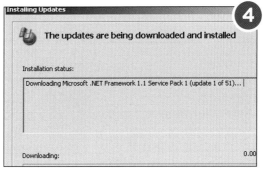

💡 **TIP**
Windows Update is great for downloading updates to a single PC that's permanently connected to the internet. If you need to install updates on several computers or a PC without internet access, you may want to download them from the Microsoft website instead. You can then burn them to a CD to share between PCs or take elsewhere.
   Using your web browser, go to *www.microsoft.com/downloads*. Click on Windows Security & Updates on the left. The most popular downloads are listed here. Click the Release Date heading to see the latest downloads, or click Advanced Search at the top to narrow the list down.

Cleaning your PC

IT'S COMMON TO give your house a good clean every spring, mow the lawn and trim the hedges. It helps keep your home and garden in good order. But what about your computer? Chances are if it's more than a year old, it's looking a bit shabby. A damp cloth on the outside may be enough to spruce it up, but you should delve into your PC's insides to give it a good clean, too.

Case fans drag dust into your case, and you may be surprised at how dirty your PC has become. While dirt you can't see may not seem a problem, it is. Dust builds up and clogs your fans, so they're less efficient at cooling. Dust also acts as an insulator, so your PC will run hotter and may crash sporadically. Here, we're encouraging you to grab a pair of Marigolds and delve into your case to clean it out. By the time you've finished, your PC will be sparkling and, more importantly, running cooler and more efficiently.

We're not going to leave it there, though. Cleaning your PC gives you a good opportunity to tidy it up. First, we'll show you how to tidy the cables. This doesn't just make the inside more pleasant to look at; it also keeps them out of the way and lets air circulate better, keeping your computer cooler. We'll also show you how to remove your processor's fan, clean it up and

reapply thermal paste, so your cooling will be as efficient as possible.

Finally, we'll cover how to clean your keyboard and monitor. Neither may sound like a priority, but a dirty keyboard is unpleasant to type on and can be a breeding ground for bacteria. Some reports have even stated that a keyboard can have more bacteria on it than a toilet seat. In addition, a dirty, dusty screen looks dull and faded compared to a carefully cleaned one.

1 Having a monitor covered in dust and dirt is distracting when you're working and it makes a mess of images and videos, but be careful when cleaning your display as harsh cleaning products can damage the protective coating on CRT and LCD screens.

You'll need foam cleaner to clean the monitor's surround and anti-static wipes to clean the screen's surface. To avoid getting the cleaner on the surface, spray the foam on a dry cloth rather than directly on the screen surround. Rub the cloth around the screen surround to make sure the plastic is completely covered in cleaner. Leave it for 15 minutes to work into the dirt. Use a new cloth to remove the cleaner; most of the dirt should come off easily, but you may have to scrub at

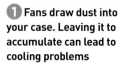

1 Fans draw dust into your case. Leaving it to accumulate can lead to cooling problems

WHAT YOU'LL NEED

In order to follow our simple instructions for a sparkling computer, you'll need the following products from *www.maplin.co.uk*. All prices include VAT.

SHOPPING LIST

1 can computer airduster	£12
1 can computer foam cleaner	£3.99
1 pot anti-static screen-cleaning wipes	£3
1 pot plastic safe wipes	£4.49
1 packet cable ties	£2.99
1 tube silver-based thermal compound	£7.99
1 bottle isopropyl alcohol	£7.29

You'll also need lint-free cloth, available from *www.diy.com* for £7.61 including VAT.

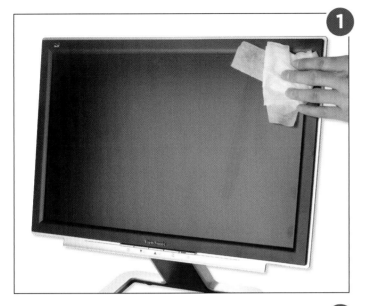

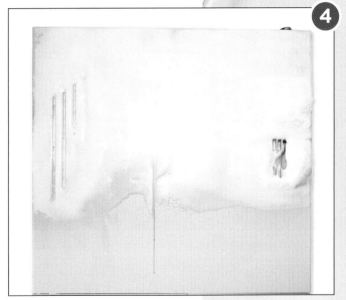

some ingrained patches. Reapply as necessary until the dirt has been removed.

Clean the screen with anti-static wipes, discarding each wipe when it becomes too dirty. To avoid leaving any smear marks, wipe the cloth vertically up and down the monitor. These wipes leave behind an anti-static film, which helps prevent dust accumulating in the future.

2 Cleaning the surface of your keyboard is quite easy; cleaning the muck from under the keys is more difficult. As this process requires

you to remove the keys, you may want to take a photo of your keybard using a digital camera, so you know where all the keys go when you put them back. You'll also need foam cleaner, a dry cloth, plastic safe wipes and the air duster. Don't spray the foam cleaner directly on the keys, as this may interfere with the switches underneath. Spray the foam on a dry cloth and apply it to the keyboard's flat surfaces. Again, leave for 15 minutes or so, then remove with the dry cloth.

It isn't possible to clean the sides of the keys or underneath them without removing them from the ▶

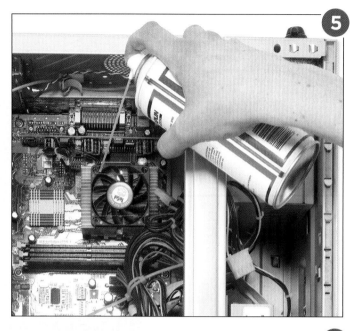

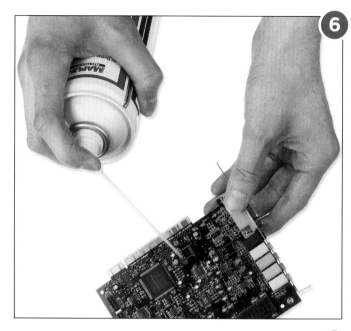

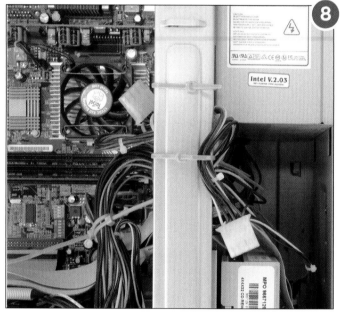

keyboard. Using a flat-bladed screwdriver, gently lever off each key. Some large keys may have extra springs or bits of metal attached to them, so don't lose these. Be extra careful when removing keys with these extra bits, as you don't want to break anything and ruin your keyboard.

3 Use the air duster to blow the dust and dirt out of the upturned keyboard. You may want to use the plastic safe wipes to get rid of any dried-on dirt. Soak the keys for around 15 minutes in a bowl with some washing-up liquid. This should get rid of most of the muck, but rub a cloth over each one to remove any residue. Any moisture left in the keys could damage the keyboard, so leave

the keys to dry completely before pressing each one back into position on the keyboard.

4 Cleaning the outside of the case is quite simple, but be careful. Don't spray the foam on to the front or rear of your PC, as it could get into your drives, power supply and ports.

Spray the foam on a cloth and apply it to the front of the case, including the optical and floppy drives. If there are any indentations around the power button or power and hard disk LEDs, you may need a cotton bud to remove dirt.

The rear of the case will be mainly metal, but rub a foam-covered cloth over the parts of the case that wrap around the rear of your PC. Use a separate cloth to wipe the case clean after you've left the foam for 15 minutes.

The sides should be more straightforward: spray the foam cleaner on to each side of the case and leave it for 15 minutes. Use a dry cloth to wipe off the cleaner and the dirt should come away easily. Reapply foam as necessary.

5 Cleaning the inside of your PC is the biggest challenge, as dust can build up in hidden areas. Take off the side of your PC and remove the expansion cards from the motherboard. If the PC is particularly dirty, you may have to remove the motherboard, hard disk and optical drives, too.

Vacuuming the motherboard is not a good idea, as there are many sensitive components protruding from the circuit board. Starting at the top, spray the air duster down over the motherboard, so the dust collects in the base of the case, or into a bin if you've removed the motherboard from the case.

Use a vacuum cleaner to remove the worst of the dust from the bottom of the case and from the processor's heatsink, fan and case fans. Finally, use the plastic safe wipes to wipe any dust from the cables inside your case.

6 The dust caked on to your expansion cards can be removed easily with the air duster. Make sure you've removed all the dust wedged underneath components such as capacitors, and check that the heatsink and fan on your graphics card are free from dust. Also, blow the air duster into your expansion cards' ports and sockets.

7 Although removing the dust from your PC's components will reduce the insulating effect and help with cooling, there are other improvements you can make to help prevent overheating. There's a thin layer of thermal compound between the processor and the heatsink, which smoothes over any imperfections in the two metal surfaces and makes sure that heat from your processor is dissipated efficiently. Eventually, thermal compound dries out and reduces the efficiency of your cooling, so it needs replacing from time to time.

Remove the heatsink from the processor as per the manufacturer's instructions. Remove the existing thermal compound using a lint-free cloth dabbed with isopropyl alcohol.

Apply a small blob of thermal compound to the top of the processor and use a piece of card to spread it evenly over the surface, so there are no visible gaps, and reattach the heatsink, making sure that it fits tightly. If not fitted properly, you run the risk of overheating.

8 There are a lot of power and data cables inside your PC, which can be messy. This makes them harder to work on and can impede airflow through your case.

Fortunately, you can solve this problem using cable ties. Find any cables that are not in use; there are normally a lot of unused power cables in a PC. Fold them up and secure them with a cable tie attached to the chassis to keep them out of the way. Now find any cables that run between roughly the same points and bunch them together before tying them up and to the chassis. Finally, find any cables that have excess amounts of slack; you may find your flat IDE ribbon cables are too long, for example. Put a kink in the cable and tie it up.

9 Case fans should draw air over your PC's components and out of the case. As the power supply already blows air out of the back of the case, your rear case fan should be oriented so that it blows air in the same direction.

If you have a front-mounted fan, make sure it's pulling cool air into the case and blowing it over your motherboard. Fans have an arrow on them that shows the direction of airflow. If any fans are mounted incorrectly, undo the mounting screws and turn the fan around before reattaching it. ▢

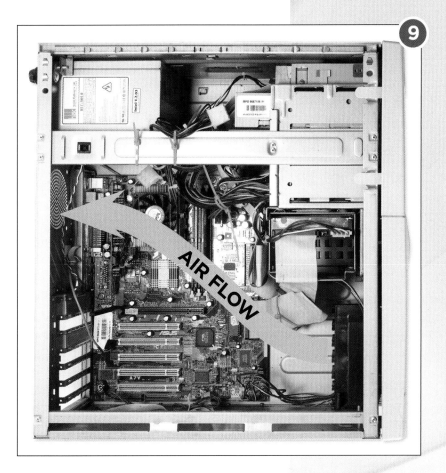

Using MSConfig to speed up your PC

AS YOU INSTALL and remove applications, your computer can become sluggish and start to slow down. One of the main causes of these problems is having too many applications and services (helper applications that do a specific job, such as monitoring for an iPod being plugged in) that start with Windows. Fortunately, Microsoft provides a tool called System Configuration that lets you control exactly what can and can't run at startup. Here, we explain how to use it.

To run the utility in Vista, click the Start menu and type msconfig, then press Enter. In Windows XP, click on the Start menu, select Run, type msconfig and press Enter. The two applications are similar, but have a couple of differences that we've pointed out below.

Vista

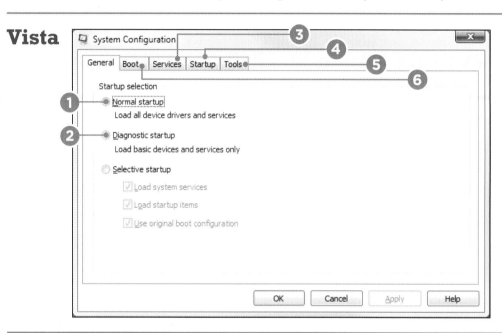

1 This is the standard setting

2 If you're having trouble, select this and Windows will start, loading only basic drivers and settings

3 This lets you choose which services to run (see the opposite page for more information)

4 This lets you choose which applications you want to run when Windows starts (see the opposite page for more information)

5 Quick access to common tools, including Event Viewer (see page 42)

6 Lets you select boot options, but you shouldn't need to change anything

XP

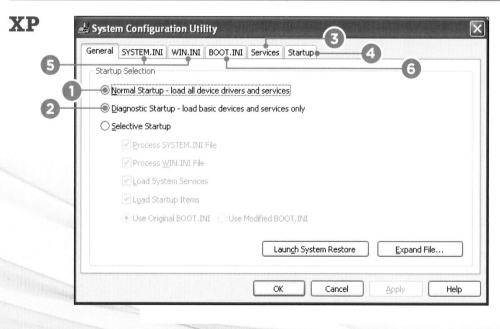

1 This is the standard setting

2 If you're having trouble, select this and Windows will start, loading only basic drivers and settings

3 This lets you choose which services to run (see the opposite page for more information)

4 Lets you choose which applications you want to run when Windows starts (see the opposite page for more information)

5 These files are no longer used

6 This lets you change boot options, but you shouldn't need to change anything here

HOW TO...
Use System Configuration

YOU CAN QUICKLY save on resources by disabling an application or service using Windows' System Configuration. For the best results, disable options one at a time and reboot your PC each time. That way you can test for problems and restore the settings if necessary.

① VIEW SERVICES
Click on the Services tab after starting System Configuration. Windows services start as Windows loads and are designed to do a specific job, such as monitoring for an iPod being connected to your computer.

Applications can rely on a particular service, so you have to be very careful about changing any settings here. In particular, you shouldn't disable any Microsoft services, as these may be needed by Windows. To make things easier, click Hide all Microsoft services.

② DISABLE SERVICES
To disable a service, click the box next to its name so that the tick is removed. You should only disable a service if you know it isn't needed. If you're not sure what a service does, type its name into Google, enclosed by double quote marks, such as "ASP.NET State Service". You're bound to find a web page that explains what the service does. Look for services that you know you don't need. For example, if you don't have an iPod or iPhone, you can disable the Apple Mobile Device service that Apple installs with iTunes. The general rule here, though, is that if you don't know what a service is for, leave it alone.

③ DISABLE STARTUP APPLICATIONS
Click on the Startup tab to view a list of applications that load when the Windows desktop appears. Click on Manufacturer to sort applications by the software developer. This makes it easier to spot, and leave alone, any Microsoft applications. Look for any manufacturers that have software you've uninstalled, then untick the box next to the application's name. You should disable any application that you know doesn't need to start with Windows. For example, Apple loads iTunes and QuickTime at startup, but both are a waste of resources. You can use Google to find out what an application does. Again, if you're not sure about an application, leave it enabled.

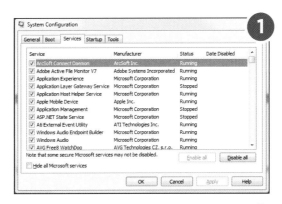

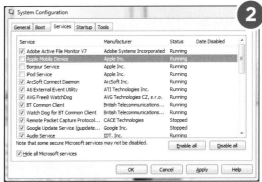

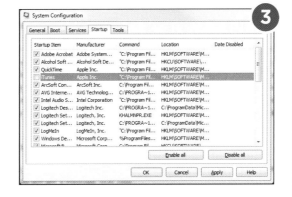

④ REBOOT AND CHECK SETTINGS
Click OK to apply the settings, and Reboot to restart your computer. When Windows loads again, you'll get a message that says, 'You have used the System Configuration Utility to make changes to the way Windows starts'. Click 'Don't show this message' to apply the changes or press OK to load System Configuration and undo any changes (don't worry, you can do this at any point).

If any changes have caused a problem, start System Configuration and click on the Services or Startup tab. Click the empty box next to an entry to re-enable it. Click OK and then Restart.

Uninterruptible power supplies

OWNING A PC isn't without its worries. Viruses try to damage your operating system, hard disks can fail and spyware can infiltrate your PC. We all know we should use a firewall and back up our files, but few of us are prepared for a failure in mains electricity. A sudden power cut could wipe out hours of work and even damage your hardware.

Fortunately, it's simple to protect your PC from power cuts. Uninterruptible power supplies (UPS), which can cost as little as £36, can also protect you from any power surges and fluctuations in voltage. Here we'll show you how to choose a UPS and ensure you've it set up correctly.

UPS devices work by storing electricity in a heavy-duty battery. In the event of a mains power failure, they immediately provide power from this battery, keeping your PC running. They also condition the electricity supply, filtering out power surges. Unlike a simple surge protector, the output voltage from most UPS devices remains stable during a temporary reduction in mains power.

You must choose a UPS that is capable of providing enough power to keep connected equipment running. In most cases, you'll want to power only a PC and monitor during a power cut, but you might also need to keep other critical peripherals running, such as an external backup device or a router.

GETTING STARTED
Before buying a UPS, calculate the total power requirements of your equipment. Most kit uses less power than the rated maximum quoted. A modern desktop PC may have a power supply rated for 500W or more, but use only around 75W when idle, rising to a maximum of 250W. A standard 17in LCD monitor uses around 30W, while a CRT may use double that. Peripherals such as routers and external hard disks consume around 10W each.

UPS manufacturers normally quote a device's maximum output in volt-amperes (VA). This figure is higher than the UPS's true power output because it includes an allowance for reactive power, which is power drawn by equipment only to be returned unconsumed to the mains. You can find a UPS's true power output, specified in watts, by looking at the manufacturer's website. Make sure that you buy a UPS with a higher power rating than the combined total for your equipment. We recommend allowing at least 20 per cent headroom, so if your equipment uses a maximum of 250W, buy a 300W UPS.

A UPS's specifications may tell you how long it will provide power. If not, you can calculate a best-case result if you know how many watt-hours (W-h) the supply's battery lasts for. This can often be found in its specifications, but you may need to work it out by multiplying the battery's voltage by its rated amp-hours (A-h). Divide the result by the power requirement you calculated for an indication of the maximum backup time you'll get.

A cheap UPS may give you just long enough to save your work and shut down your PC in a power cut. If you need to keep working, or you're serving files or a website from your PC, you may need it to survive longer. If your PC is often left running unattended, choose a UPS that can communicate with your PC via a USB or COM port. The UPS's software will detect a power cut and shut down your PC safely before its battery runs out.

Make sure the UPS has the right number and type of power sockets. Some sockets provide uninterrupted power, while others provide surge protection only and will switch off in a power cut.

All UPS devices come with a warranty that covers connected equipment. The best warranties also provide cover for loss of data.

1 PHONE SOCKET Protects your modem/router or fax device from a power surge through the phone line.

2 UPS SOCKETS Provide conditioned, surge-protected electricity and continue to work in a power cut. Use only for essential equipment such as your PC and monitor.

3 SURGE-PROTECTED ONLY SOCKET Provides surge-protected electricity but stops working in a power cut. Suitable for non-essential equipment such as a laser printer.

4 USB AND SERIAL PORTS Connect your computer here to allow the UPS software to monitor system power and safely shut down the PC in a power cut. You'll need a matching port on your PC.

5 STATUS LEDS (ON the FRONT) All UPS devices use LEDs and beeps to indicate their status. Your manual will explain what these mean.

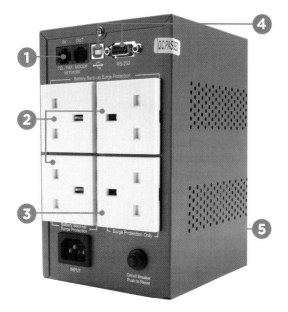

HOW TO...
Set up a UPS

① PHYSICAL INSTALLATION

A UPS is usually best positioned on the floor, but leave space for ventilation as it can get warm while charging or discharging. UPS devices emit a strong electromagnetic field that may interfere with your monitor and could damage a magnetic storage device such as a hard disk MP3 player. Position your UPS at least 30cm away from sensitive devices, plugging it directly into an earthed wall socket, not a multiple plug adaptor.

Plug your PC, monitor and any essential peripherals into the UPS sockets. If you want to stay connected to the internet in a power cut, make sure you plug your modem or router into the UPS. Plug non-essential devices such as printers or scanners into surge-protected sockets, if there are any. If there aren't, buy a simple surge-protected multi-way adaptor for them. If the UPS has a surge-protected phone socket or network port, simply daisy-chain your present connections through it. If required, connect the UPS to your PC using the USB or COM port.

Once everything is plugged in, switch on the UPS. Consult the accompanying manual to ensure the status lights aren't indicating any problems. If everything is OK, power up your PC. If your UPS has a data link to your PC and came with its own software, continue to Step 2; if you have a simple device with no software, go straight to Step 3.

② SOFTWARE INSTALLATION

Follow the manufacturer's instructions to install the software that came with your UPS. Check that the software has recognised the UPS correctly. You can use the software to monitor your UPS's status while it charges.

You can configure the software to shut down your PC automatically in a power cut. Most software will let you select how this happens. The most common option is to shut down the PC immediately upon detecting a power cut. This conserves battery power should you need it later, but remember that other connected peripherals may still be consuming some power.

The alternative is to keep the PC running for as long as possible then shut it down just before the battery expires. Whichever option you choose, you can override the automatic shutdown if required.

③ CONFIGURING YOUR PC

For your PC to power off successfully, you must ensure there's no software running that prevents a clean shutdown. Right-click on the desktop and select Properties, click on the Screen Saver tab and then Power. Go to the Hibernate tab and check that the hibernation option is ticked. On the Power Schemes tab, change the drop-down setting so the system will hibernate after five minutes. Apply your changes and leave the PC until it hibernates, then power it back on and return it to its previous hibernation settings.

If your PC doesn't hibernate cleanly, run Help and Support from the Start menu. Type shutdown into the box, select the Startup and Shutdown Troubleshooter and follow the instructions.

To reduce the risk of losing data when you power off, make sure your applications are set up to make regular autosaves of your work.

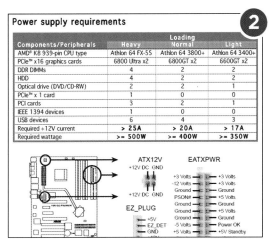

Power supply requirements			
		Loading	
Components/Peripherals	Heavy	Normal	Light
AMD® K8 939-pin CPU type	Athlon 64 FX-55	Athlon 64 3800+	Athlon 64 3400+
PCIe™ x16 graphics cards	6800 Ultra x2	6800GT x2	6600GT x2
DDR DIMMs	4	2	2
HDD	4	2	2
Optical drive (DVD/CD-RW)	2	2	1
PCIe™ x 1 card	1	0	0
PCI cards	3	2	1
IEEE 1394 devices	1	0	0
USB devices	6	4	3
Required +12V current	> 25A	> 20A	> 17A
Required wattage	>= 500W	>= 400W	>= 350W

TIP

If your UPS has normal three-pin square plugs, use one of the battery-backed plugs for a lamp. In the event of a power failure you'll be able to use its light to shut down your PC or perform other jobs, even if it's the middle of the night.

Avoiding viruses

BY FOLLOWING THESE rules, you can drastically reduce the chances of downloading a virus.

UPDATE YOUR SYSTEM

Viruses often work by attacking security holes in your PC's operating system, which will most likely be Windows XP or Vista. When Microsoft becomes aware of these holes, it creates programs to plug them. These applications are known as updates, and Windows can download and install them automatically (see page 89). If you keep your system up to date, you massively reduce the risk of a virus infection.

Windows 98 and earlier versions are no longer supported by Microsoft, which means that even if it discovers a security hole in an old version of the operating system, it won't fix it. For this reason, you should upgrade to Vista. Support for XP will end within the next two years so, you should think about changing to Vista sooner rather than later. Alternatively, you could wait for Windows 7, which will probably be launched around the time that XP's support comes to an end.

IGNORE ATTACHMENTS FROM STRANGERS

Viruses may come attached to emails. These attachments may claim to be updates from Microsoft, interesting video clips, electronic greetings cards or any number of other things you might want to open. Unless you're absolutely sure that an attachment is genuine, don't run it.

Avoiding infected attachments is not foolproof. Even if you only ever run attachments that come from people you know, some viruses will still be able to trick you on occasion. This is because, when they infect a system, they read the victim's email address book. A virus may then send copies of itself to everyone in that list. The end result is that your inbox contains infected email messages that appear to have come from friends and family.

If you're unsure about an attachment, there's no harm in contacting the sender and asking about it. A hacker or virus will not reply and, if you get a confused reply, you can delete the message safe in the knowledge that it's probably infected.

AVOID THE NET'S DARK CORNERS

Although viruses can appear on legitimate websites, they are more common in the seedier parts of the internet. If you make efforts to avoid pornographic, peer-to-peer (P2P) file-sharing and piracy sites, you'll reduce your exposure to viruses. Websites that offer cracks, used to break the copy protection of commercial software such as Norton AntiVirus, Adobe Photoshop and Microsoft Office, are also best avoided.

P2P services may offer access to illegally copied music and movies, as well as software. Any of these files could be infected. Downloading them not only puts you at risk of prosecution, but puts your PC in danger of contracting a virus as well. And if that virus leaks your personal or financial details to hackers, you'll soon wish you'd stumped up the cash instead of opting for pirated goods.

USE A STANDARD ACCOUNT

When you log into Windows, you'll usually need to use a username and password. Unfortunately, in most cases, you'll log in using a very powerful account called Administrator. This is not all bad – it means that you'll be able to make changes to your PC's settings, install software and so on. However, it also means that any virus you encounter stands a better chance of breaking into your system.

It is much safer to log in using Windows Vista's Standard user account. In Windows XP, this account is called the Limited user account. In both cases, you're restricted in what you can do, so you

1 Update your system and it will become immune to many of the threats on the internet

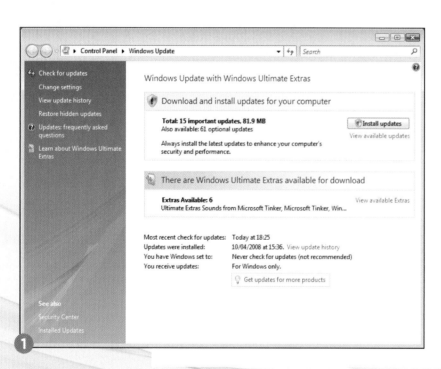

won't easily be able to install software or change important system settings. The useful side effect is that viruses will find it harder to crack your computer, too.

INSTALL ANTI-VIRUS SOFTWARE
If you've followed all the above advice, you'll reduce the chances of being infected by a virus significantly. However, there's always a chance that one will get through. This is when you'll be glad that you installed some anti-virus software.

Anti-virus software keeps a constant eye on your computer and, if it detects any harmful software, tries to prevent it from running and installing. For advice on installing an anti-virus program, see page 100.

INSTALL A FIREWALL
Firewalls prevent network worms from attacking your PC. If you have a broadband connection, you probably have a firewall already, as many routers include one. Other firewalls are software programs that you install just like an anti-virus application. In fact, many internet security programs include both a firewall and anti-virus software in one package.

The advantage of software firewalls is that they can prevent viruses and other unauthorised programs from sending information from your computer to the internet. This helps prevent spyware from stealing your personal information.

CHANGE YOUR BROWSER'S SETTINGS
It is possible to change some advanced settings in your web browser, which is most likely Internet Explorer, to improve your security when you access the web. However, this is a pain to do.

Unless you're an expert, you'll probably find it difficult to work out which settings should be changed. Even if you get this right, you'll find that

some websites will refuse to work properly. These will probably include your online bank and other important services.

If you really want to lock down your computer, follow the advice provided by Microsoft at *www. microsoft.com/protect/computer/advanced/ browsing.mspx*.

DON'T CONNECT TO THE INTERNET
It may seem odd advice in today's connected world, but you don't always need to connect your PC to the internet, and in some cases you shouldn't. If you have to use an old version of Windows for some reason – perhaps because later versions don't work with some of your peripherals, for example – you can continue to use it safely as long as you don't connect it to the internet.

If yours is one of the many households in the UK with more than one computer, consider using one computer for internet activities such as browsing the web and reading email and another for word processing, image editing and creating your home videos. You don't need an online connection for any of these tasks, so decide whether or not you really need to allow this computer to access the internet.

② Shun pirated software and you'll avoid the nasty surprises that often come included

③ A firewall will repel attacks from the web and stop viruses from sending your personal information to hackers

④ Installing a good anti-virus program provides an essential layer of protection for your computer

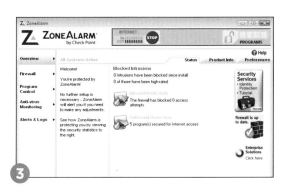

Installing an anti-virus program

BEFORE YOU INSTALL an anti-virus program, make sure you don't already have one. Running more than one anti-virus application simultaneously will slow down your computer horribly and may even cause it to crash. Check the icons at the bottom-right of the screen, in the Notification area, to see what security products are already running.

We've used Norton AntiVirus for the purposes of this article, but the principles are roughly the same for any anti-virus application.

1 If your choice of anti-virus software is available online, visit its website and download the installation file to your hard disk.

2 You will almost certainly be asked to register or activate the software. This usually means entering a long series of numbers and letters. You may need to have your PC connected to the net.

3 Almost every anti-virus program relies on a regular supply of information from the company that created it. These updates allow the

software to stay abreast of developments and detect new viruses and other threats. The first thing you should do once the anti-virus program is running on your computer, therefore, is update it. Some programs will do this automatically, while others will ask. Always agree to this.

4 After the program has downloaded its updates, you may need to restart the computer. In some cases, the application will then download even more updates and require another restart. This may be tedious, but it won't take long and you will then be able to run the first anti-virus scan on your system.

If you're lucky, the program will offer to do this for you. Otherwise, you may need to find the appropriate option. This might be as easy as right-clicking the program's icon in the notification area and choosing Full Scan or Scan Computer.

5 Even if your computer is free of viruses, the anti-virus program will almost certainly claim to find some problems. It will probably ask you

how it should treat these threats, which might be as innocent as some small, harmless text files left on your hard disk by your favourite websites. These cookies are rarely anything to worry about and, if you let the program delete them, you may find you have problems logging into important websites such as your online bank. Allow the program to delete anything more serious.

6 When you close your anti-virus application, usually by clicking the red cross at the top-right part of the window, it will continue to run in the background. You may want to change some of the settings before you leave it to protect your computer.

Generally an anti-virus program will delete or quarantine threats when it finds them, but often it will alert you first and may even ask you what to do. You can usually set up the program to manage these situations automatically.

7 Anti-virus programs can be adjusted to be more or less aggressive. The default settings ought to be good enough for everyday use, but you can usually tune its detection engine's sensitivity. The more sensitive it is, the slower your PC will run. Reducing its sensitivity too much will improve the PC's overall speed but increases the risk that viruses will be able to infect it.

Norton AntiVirus has three scan profiles: Full Scan; Standard Trust and High Trust. Full scan is more thorough but slower.

8 Automatic updates are crucial to an anti-virus program, which needs to stay completely abreast of the latest developments. Although you'll want your application to be able to detect new viruses, sometimes you'll want to turn off its update system. If you're temporarily using an expensive and slow mobile broadband connection, for example, it's reasonable to turn off updates for that session.

CUSTOMISING YOUR SECURITY SUITE

Internet security suites contain lots of useful features, but you won't need all of them. Although the following settings can add to your computer's protection, you can disable one or more of them to reclaim a little speed if you need to.

EMAIL SCANNER

Disable this if you use a web-based email service such as Google Mail or Yahoo! Mail.

ANTI-SPAM

Disable this if you have an anti-spam service.

PARENTAL CONTROLS

If you're already using Vista's Parental Controls, disable your security suite's controls. Alternatively, leave them running but disable Vista's system.

SCHEDULED SCANNING

A good security suite should prevent a threat from entering your system. If you keep your anti-virus program up to date, there's little point in scanning your computer regularly.

Chapter 8

Into the BIOS

BEFORE YOU CAN reinstall an operating system on your PC, you'll need to change a few settings in the BIOS. The BIOS is where you can configure the speed of your processor and memory, make settings such as a system password and choose the time at which the PC boots up every day. In this chapter, we'll show you how to access the BIOS and make the appropriate changes.

Into the BIOS

THE BIOS IS part of the motherboard, and is arguably one of its most important components. If it gets physically damaged or corrupted by a virus, there's a good chance that you won't be able to use your computer at all.

Thankfully, the chances of either of these happening is minimal: it's much more common that the wrong settings will have been made in the BIOS. Fortunately, the BIOS is simple to use, and relatively easy to understand.

BIOSes have a limited amount of memory, which is used to store the settings. This memory keeps the settings – including the date and time – as long as the motherboard's battery has charge. However, despite huge advances in almost every other aspect of a computer, the BIOS has

remained virtually unchanged in the way it looks and works for around 25 years.

There are only a few major BIOS makers, including Award and Phoenix, and most BIOSes look very similar. However, you need to bear in mind that yours may have different options to those shown over the next few pages. So, while the following steps may not match up with the options you have, it shouldn't be difficult to work out how to modify our instructions to apply them to what you see on your screen.

Initially, you may find that you don't need to make many changes to get to a stage where you can install your operating system. Here, we'll show you what all the options are for, so you can come back later and tweak everything to your liking.

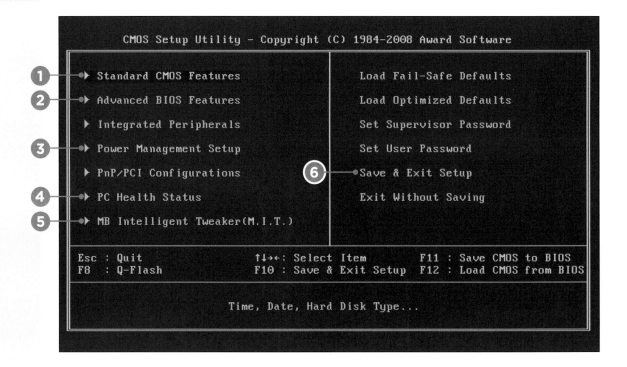

❶ Contains settings for date, time, hard disks, optical and floppy drives

❷ Here you can set the boot order, passwords and processor features

❸ Head for power settings, including sleep mode and devices that can wake up the PC

❹ Information on temperatures, fans and voltages

❺ Here's where you make advanced processor and memory settings

❻ When you've made changes, choose this option to save and reboot

HOW TO...
Edit the BIOS

① GET INTO THE BIOS

Many of the latest motherboards feature graphic splash screens, which hide the traditional black and white text. We've used a Gigabyte motherboard here. As with most boards, you press the Delete key to access the BIOS. While some BIOSes use alternative keys, such as F1, F2 or F10, it should be easy to spot which you need to use, as it will be shown somewhere obvious onscreen.

Push the power button, wait for the POST (Power-On Self Test) screen to appear and press the appropriate key to enter the BIOS. If you miss the POST screen, press Ctrl-Alt-Del to restart the computer.

② THE MAIN SCREEN

The main BIOS screen will now appear. Even if yours doesn't look like this, the menu options should be similar. To navigate, use the cursor keys. On most BIOSes, you can select an option by pressing Enter or the right cursor key. Pressing Esc will return you to the POST screen, while F10 jumps to the Save & Exit confirmation prompt.

③ SET DATE AND TIME

Let's work through the main menu options in order. One of the first things you need to do is to set the correct date and time, as Windows uses this information. Standard CMOS Features should already be selected – it's highlighted in red – so you simply need to press Enter.

Again, you navigate through the settings using the cursor keys. All changeable settings are shown in yellow, while those that aren't are in light blue. Set the correct time and date by highlighting the part you want to change, and alter its value by pressing the + or – key. Alternatively, you can use the Page Up and Page Down keys.

④ CONFIGURE HARD DISK

In the IDE listing, you should see your hard disk and optical drive. Most motherboards don't differentiate between PATA and SATA drives, simply referring to them as IDE. All the entries marked 'None' are the PATA and SATA ports, to which no drives are connected. During the POST, all of these are checked to see if there's anything connected, but to save a few seconds of boot time you can disable the unused channels.

To do this, highlight a channel, press Enter, then select the name of the channel in the screen that appears – in this case, IDE Channel 0 Slave. Press Enter again and a window will appear with the options None, Auto or Manual. Change the setting ⟩

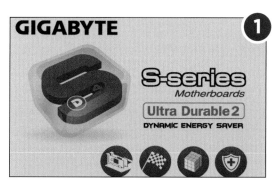

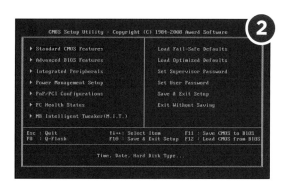

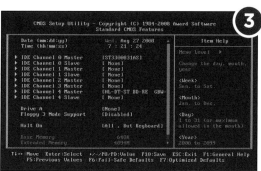

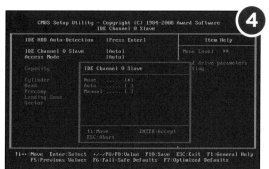

⑨ TIP

If you make a mistake or your settings aren't working, use the **Load Fail-Safe Defaults** option to reset the BIOS.

from Auto to None, and this channel will no longer be checked at boot time. If you ever want to connect a drive to this channel, remember to re-enable it by changing it back to Auto.

⑤ CONFIGURE FLOPPY DISK
Press Enter to accept the change and return to the Standard CMOS Features menu. It's unlikely that you'll have fitted a floppy drive in your PC, so highlight Drive A and press Enter. This will open a window where you can select the type of floppy drive. Here, you can see proof that the BIOS hasn't changed for a long time, as there are entries for 5¼in floppy disk drives, despite the fact that this motherboard was brand new in summer 2008. Select None or 1.44M, 3.5" if you've installed a drive, and press Enter to accept.

On the right-hand side of the Standard CMOS Features screen, you'll see contextual help, which provides terse information on the setting you've highlighted. Usually, this is fairly unhelpful, so it's a good idea to have your motherboard's manual handy in case you need to refer to it.

⑥ SET UP BOOT DEVICE
Press Esc to return to the main BIOS menu, and go to the second heading: Advanced BIOS Features. Depending on your particular BIOS, you may find processor and memory settings here, but we'll get to those in Step 13, as they're under a different heading in our BIOS. The most important settings in this menu are the Boot Device options. You need to ensure that the first boot device is set

to CD-ROM, since the operating system is most likely to be on a CD. The BIOS doesn't differentiate between types of optical drive, so CD-ROM refers to all types of drive, including DVD and Blu-ray drives. Press Enter to accept your choice, and then ensure that the second boot device is set to hard disk. This is necessary because, once you've installed an operating system, the hard disk becomes the bootable device.

⑦ MORE ADVANCED FEATURES
The rest of the Advanced BIOS Features vary from motherboard to motherboard, but you may want to check the other options to make sure you're happy with their default values. The CPU Thermal Monitor, for example, can be disabled if you don't want the BIOS to keep tabs on your processor's temperature. However, it's advisable to enable this to prevent overheating and possible damage to your processor.

Other options include the ability to disable the POST splash screen, and to choose which graphics card is initialised first: an integrated chip or a graphics card in the PCI Express slot.

⑧ CONFIGURE PORTS
Press Esc to return to the main menu, then choose Integrated Peripherals. This will show a list of the main components on your motherboard, including SATA and RAID ports, USB ports, audio, FireWire, network adaptors and legacy ports such as serial and parallel ports. It's good practice to disable anything you know

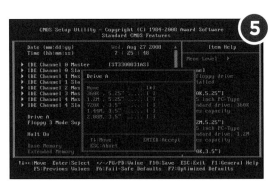

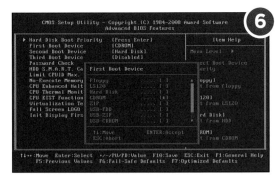

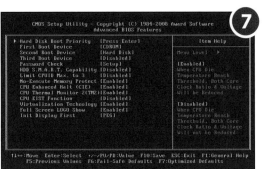

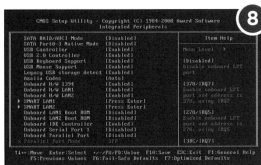

you're not going to us e. On this motherboard, like many modern boards with Intel chipsets, the audio chip is somewhat mysteriously called Azalia Codec. This is a case where the motherboard manual may be useful.

9 POWER MANAGEMENT

Next, go into Power Management Setup. It's crucial that you make the right choice for ACPI Suspend Type, as this will determine whether Windows' Sleep mode works correctly or not. Usually, you'll see two options: S1 and S3. You want S3, which is the Suspend-to-RAM option.

S1 provides little in the way of power saving, and doesn't power down all the main components. S3, by contrast, turns off everything apart from the memory, so the processor, graphics card and other power-hungry components are switched off.

When you tell Windows to go into Sleep mode, the current state of open programs is saved to memory, enabling Windows to restart in just a few seconds when you push the power button.

10 POWER ON CONTROL

Other settings in Power Management Setup include Soft-Off by PWR-BTTN. This sets how long you have to hold down the PC's power button before it switches off. The options usually range from instant to four seconds. We'd advise setting this to the latter to avoid losing work if you accidentally knock the power button.

Other options here include Resume by Alarm, which lets you specify when your PC switches on every day, either on weekdays or at weekends. Usually, you can choose only one option and can't set a different power-on time for weekdays and weekends.

Finally, there are options that determine which devices can wake up the computer, including the mouse, keyboard and network adaptor. The latter is often called Power On by Ring.

11 PC HEALTH

Return to the main menu and then choose PC Health Status. This is where you can view voltages, temperatures and fan speeds. For most, voltages won't be of interest, but temperatures will be. There may be more than two, but you will certainly see CPU Temperature and System Temperature. The former will usually be quite a lot higher than the latter; 30ºC to 60ºC is a normal idle temperature for a processor. System temperature is the ambient temperature inside the computer's case, and if it's significantly higher than 30ºC, you may want to install an extra case fan or two.

Fan speeds aren't particularly interesting, but Smart FAN options can be useful, as they can vary the fan speed according to temperature. Usually this makes your PC quieter when it's not doing anything demanding.

12 MONITOR TEMPERATURES

One of the most useful settings in PC Health Status is the CPU Warning Temperature. Press Enter when this is highlighted and you'll see a window with a selection of temperatures. The one

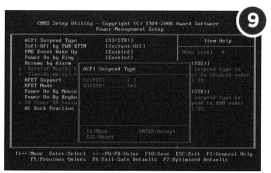

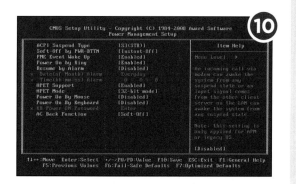

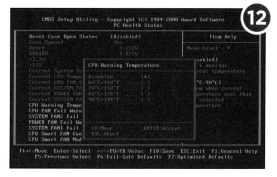

TIP

The temperature monitor can be useful in diagnosing problems with your computer: hot PCs will crash more often than cool ones.

you choose will need to be based on the processor you have, as some run much cooler than others and you don't want a buzzer going off when it's running at a normal temperature. Our processor's idle temperature is around 55°C, so 80°C is a sensible warning temperature.

13 EXAMINE PROCESSOR SPEED

Somewhere in the main BIOS menu, there should be an item for processor and memory settings. Names vary, but it shouldn't be hard to find. Options for altering settings will also vary from those you see here, but the essential ones are always present. Check that your processor's speed is correctly set. Here, our Core 2 Duo E8500 is correctly showing under CPU Frequency as 3.16GHz (333x9.5). The part in brackets is the front side bus speed (also known as CPU Host Clock or Frequency) and the multiplier (also known as CPU Clock Ratio). Multiplying the two gives you the processor's speed. If you know the frequency at which your processor should run and this figure matches what you see on this screen, you don't need to worry about the figures in brackets.

14 ADJUST PROCESSOR SPEED

If your processor's speed isn't showing correctly, set it manually by altering the CPU Host Frequency (MHz). Highlight this field, which represents the front side bus speed, and press Enter (you may first have to enable this field by choosing Enabled under CPU Host Clock Control). Type in the speed, which will either be 333 or

400 for Intel processors, and 200MHz for AMD processors. If you're not sure, check the specification of your particular model. Press Enter and the change should be reflected in the CPU Frequency field.

15 ADJUST PROCESSOR MULTIPLIER

If the CPU Clock Ratio is showing the wrong value, you may be able to change it. Highlight this field and press Enter. You'll either see a list of the available multipliers, or a box in which to type the ratio number. Enter the right one for your processor. If the value you want isn't shown, your motherboard may not fully support the processor and run at a slower speed.

It isn't normally possible to alter the multiplier since most Intel and AMD processors have locked clock ratios. Only enthusiast processors such as AMD's Black Editions and Intel's Extreme Editions tend to have unlocked multipliers. Some Intel motherboards also force you to type an integer into the ratio box, and if you need a 0.5 multiplier, you have to select this in the next field down.

16 BIOS VERSION

You may be able to upgrade your BIOS to a newer version to add support for newer processors. Visit the website of your motherboard manufacturer to find out if there's a new version. This is often listed in under Firmware.

To check which BIOS version your motherboard is currently running, save and exit the BIOS, and restart the PC. When the POST screen appears,

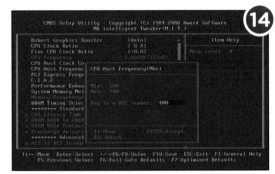

look for a version number; it's usually at the top or bottom of the screen – we've highlighted it in the picture below. Version numbers aren't shown on graphical splash screens, so you should hit Tab to show the POST screen.

17 SET MEMORY SPEED

It's unlikely that you'll have a problem with your processor's speed being detected incorrectly. More common is that memory speeds are wrongly set. The BIOS usually defaults to Auto settings to ensure overall system reliability, but this can often lead to the memory running slower than it can. Memory has a headline speed figure, in MHz, such as 667, 800 or 1,066. But there are other speed ratings that can affect performance, including those shown here: CAS Latency; RAS-to-CAS Delay; RAS Precharge and Precharge Delay (tRAS).

18 SET MEMORY TIMINGS

Many memory modules have these timings printed in that order on stickers, so look to see what yours is rated at. It'll be something like 4-4-4-12 or 2-2-2-5. If the values in the BIOS are higher than these, change them manually. Highlight each in turn, press Enter and change it from Auto to the value you want. Higher numbers indicate slower performance, as they relate to times.

As with all advanced BIOS settings, we'd advise changing only one setting at a time and rebooting to see if everything is working correctly. If you make several changes and the PC doesn't boot, you won't know which one caused it.

19 OVERCLOCK YOUR PC

Scroll down the list of processor and memory options, and you should find voltage settings. We'd recommend leaving these at their default values, as changing them can damage your hardware. They're here for those that want to overclock some components, primarily the processor and memory.

Overclocking makes components run faster than their stated speed, which can give extra performance for free, but it usually comes with the trade-off of reliability. When you overclock a component, you'll usually need to increase its voltage slightly to increase stability. Many motherboards have automatic overclocking options, so you don't need to change frequency and voltage settings yourself. Look for a menu that has options such as 2%, 5%, 10% or Standard, Turbo, Extreme.

20 SAVE YOUR SETTINGS

The rest of the options in the main menu are self-explanatory and let you set passwords – for the BIOS or the whole PC – and exit the BIOS having saved your settings. The other menu items are Load Fail-Safe Defaults and Load Optimized Defaults. The first sets all BIOS options to their original values, which should ensure that the PC will boot and will prevent stability problems. You should use this option if you made changes to the BIOS that caused your PC to stop booting. Optimized Defaults loads settings to run the PC at optimal performance, but if you've followed these steps, you'll have the optimal setup.

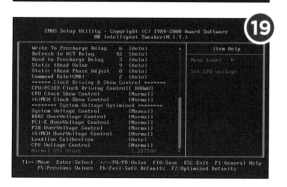

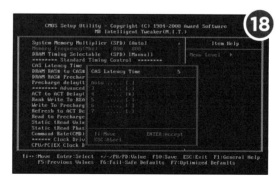

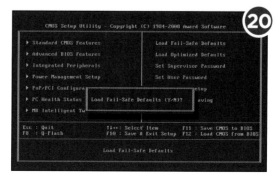

⊙ TIP
Memory is often detected incorrectly by the BIOS, so check the settings before continuing.

Chapter 9

Operating systems

THERE ARE TIMES when a computer is so broken that you have no choice but to reinstall Windows. In this chapter, we'll show you how.

You'll need your original Windows disc to hand to follow these steps. As well as simply restoring Windows, you can perform a repair installation, which will keep your current settings and get your computer working again.

If you're installing from scratch, don't forget to download drivers for your hardware (see page 10). Once you've completed your repair, you should follow our backup guide to take a complete copy of your system and files (see page 84).

HOW TO...
Install or repair Vista

① START YOUR COMPUTER
Turn on your PC and put the Windows Vista DVD into the optical drive. If you have a new hard disk, the Vista installation routine will load automatically, but if you're using an old hard disk with an operating system already on it, press any key when prompted. If you don't, your old operating system will start and you'll have to reset your PC to start the setup wizard.

Your computer will take a few minutes to start the installation routine, so don't worry if you just see a blank page for a bit.

② CHOOSE YOUR LANGUAGE OPTIONS
The first screen that appears will ask you to choose which language you want to use. Select English from the drop-down menu. Select English (United Kingdom) as the time and currency format. This should automatically change the keyboard or input method to UK. If it doesn't, select UK from the third drop-down menu. Click Next to continue.

③ INSTALL VISTA
On the next screen, click 'What to know before installing Windows' if you want additional information about Windows Vista. The 'Repair your computer' link needs to be used only if you've already installed Vista and are having problems with the installation. Otherwise, just click the Install now button.

④ ENTER YOUR PRODUCT KEY
Windows will prompt you to type your product key, which is inside the box in which your copy of Windows came. Leave the 'Automatically activate Windows when I'm online' box ticked to let Windows activate itself when you connect to the internet. If you're performing a new installation, enter the key now. Don't enter your product key if you're doing a Repair installation, otherwise you may run into problems, and click No any time that you're prompted to enter a key. Don't tick the Automatically activate Windows box, either.

Click Next, and click the tick box on the next screen to confirm that you've read the licence agreement and click Next again. If you didn't enter your product key, select which version of Vista you have (Home Premium, Business, Ultimate and so on). Select 'I have selected the edition of Windows that I purchased' and click Next to continue.

BEFORE YOU BEGIN
A Repair installation won't fix every problem. If your computer's not working properly, it's best either to perform a fresh installation of Vista using these instructions, or restore a backup (see page 84).

If you're going to do a Repair installation, your Windows disc needs to contain the same version of service pack as your PC. If it doesn't, you'll need to create a slipstreamed disc (see, http://tinyurl.com/slipstreamvista).

5 CHOOSE TYPE OF INSTALLATION

You'll be asked to choose if you want to upgrade an old copy of Windows or run a new Custom installation. If you're repairing your copy of Vista, click Upgrade. If you're installing a fresh copy of Vista, select the Custom option.

6 SELECT HARD DISK

Your hard disk should automatically be detected by Windows Vista. If it isn't, click on the Load Driver button and insert the CD, USB key or floppy disk with the relevant driver. You should need to do this only if you're using RAID or you have a brand new motherboard that Windows doesn't recognise.

From the list of disks, select the one on which you want Windows to be installed. If you've installed Windows before, you'll need to select the first partition in the list and click Next.

If you're installing to a new disk, select it (this is usually Disk 0). If you click Next, Windows will format the entire disk automatically. However, it's best to create at least two partitions: one for Windows, and a smaller one for backups, drivers and other files you want permanently.

Click Advanced options and then New to add a new partition. You have to select the size of the partition in megabytes (1,024MB equals 1GB). Generally, we'd recommend leaving at least 40GB (40,960MB) for the second partition. So subtract the size of second partition you want from the figure in the box, and enter this. Click Apply. Select Disk 0 Unallocated Space, click New and click Apply. You now have two partitions.

7 FORMAT DISKS

To make things easier once you've started Windows, you should format your partitions now. Select Partition 1 and click Format. Click OK in the warning box. You'll see an hourglass for a few moments while the disk is formatted. Repeat these steps for the second disk. When that has been formatted, click Next.

8 INSTALLING WINDOWS FILES

Next, Windows will automatically copy system files and install the necessary drivers to get your PC working on the first partition that you created. This process can take up to 30 minutes, and your computer will restart several times during ▶

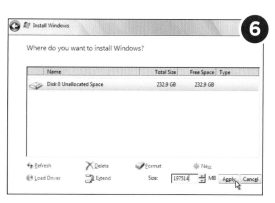

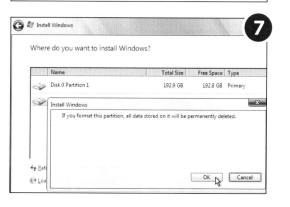

💡 **TIP**
The blue arrow in the top-left of the installation screens allows you to go back to a previous step.

the operation. There's nothing for you to worry about at this point; just sit back and let Windows do its job until the system starts for the first time.

⑨ SET UP A USERNAME

When your computer starts Windows Vista for the first time, you'll be asked to enter a username and password. While the password is optional, if you want to protect your files from unwanted attention and ensure that only authorised users can access your PC, it's vital that you have one. Type in a username and password, and then click Next.

Give your computer a meaningful name and then choose which desktop background you'd like. Click Next to continue.

⑩ PROTECT WINDOWS

Windows will now ask whether you want to turn on Windows Updates automatically. The best option is to use the recommended settings, so click that box. Next, set the date and time of your computer. Make sure your time zone has been set correctly. If you chose your location as UK in the Windows installation routine, then the time zone will be set to GMT by default. Click Next and then Start to launch Windows.

⑪ START WINDOWS

Windows will now perform some tests on your computer's performance. These will take around five minutes to complete. Once it's finished, you'll be presented with the login screen. If you set a password, you'll have to enter it now and press Enter. Windows will prepare your desktop for its first use and log you on.

You'll now see the Welcome Center, which gives you quick access to information about Vista and also short cuts to common tasks, such as adding new users. The next time you start Windows, you'll see a box, which you can tick if you don't want to see the Welcome Center again. You can now remove the Windows Vista installation DVD.

⑫ INSTALL MOTHERBOARD DRIVERS

Although Windows is now working, you still need to install all the relevant drivers to make sure that everything will work smoothly. The first place to start is with your motherboard's drivers. If you downloaded these earlier, insert the USB key or disc you saved them to. If you couldn't do this, insert the driver disc and follow the onscreen instructions. You'll need to download the updated drivers later when you're connected to the internet (see page 10), and then follow these instructions.

For each driver you downloaded, run the associated file. It's best to start with the chipset driver, but the order afterwards doesn't matter. If Windows displays any warning messages, just click OK. Be careful, as some files you download are actually just archive files that extract the

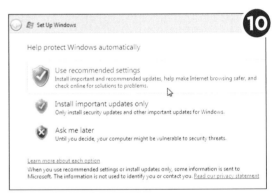

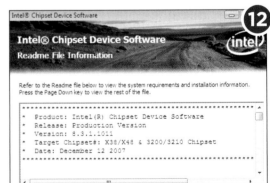

actual driver files on to your hard disk. If this is the case, navigate to the folder the files were extracted to and run the Setup program that you find there. You'll probably need to restart your computer after each driver installation.

13 INSTALL GRAPHICS CARD DRIVERS

Windows will install its own graphics drivers for any onboard or dedicated cards that you have. These are good enough to run Windows, but you won't be able to play games properly. Instead, you'll need to install the graphics drivers.

Both ATI and Nvidia provide a single driver package. You simply have to run the file that you downloaded. If you couldn't download the drivers earlier, you need to insert the bundled CD, but remember to download newer drivers later on.

Restart your computer after the graphics drivers have been installed. Right-click on the desktop, select Personalize, then Display Properties and change your display resolution to match your monitor's native resolution.

14 INSTALL OTHER PERIPHERALS

You can now install the other peripherals that you've added to your PC. Install the relevant driver files for each device that's plugged into your motherboard. For USB devices, you need to install the driver file first and, when prompted, connect the device to a USB port. If you're in any doubt, you should read the manual that came with your

peripheral. If you've installed a wireless adaptor, make sure that you connect it to your wireless network and follow the provided instructions.

15 INSTALL SERVICE PACK 1

When everything else is installed, you should install Windows Vista Service Pack 1, unless the installation disc you used included this, in which case you can skip to the final step.

To install Service Pack 1, first connect to the internet. The easiest way to force it to install is to go to *http://tinyurl.com/vistaservicepack1*. Click Download and save the file to your hard disk. When it's finished, run the file and follow the wizard. Service Pack 1 will take around an hour to install and will restart your computer when necessary.

16 RUN WINDOWS UPDATE

Click on the Start menu, type Windows Update and click the entry that appears. Click the Check for Updates button, and Windows will connect to Microsoft's update server and detect which updates you need.

Click on 'View available updates' and have a look at the list. There will be some that have been preselected as important updates, but there are also some optional ones, including even newer drivers for your hardware. Select what you'd like to update and then click Install.

Once they're installed, your job is done.

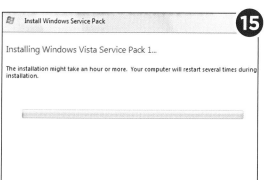

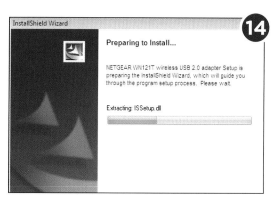

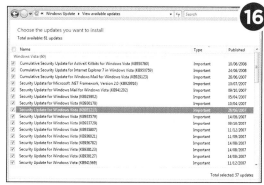

HOW TO...
Install or repair XP

① START YOUR COMPUTER
Turn your PC on and put the Windows XP CD into your optical drive. If you're using a brand new hard disk, the XP installation routine will load automatically. If you're using an old hard disk that already has an operating system on it, you need to press any key when prompted onscreen. If you don't, your old operating system will start and you'll have to reset your PC to load the installer.

Your computer will take a few minutes to start the installation routine properly, so don't worry if you see a blank page for a bit.

② ADD ADDITIONAL DRIVES
If you've got a RAID controller or hard disk that's not detected (you'll discover this later on and may need to restart the installation routine), you need to add additional drivers. When prompted, press F6. Windows will continue copying files, but after a couple of minutes, a screen will ask what drivers you want to add. Press S to specify additional devices. You'll need to have the files on a floppy disk and a floppy disk drive, as Windows XP can't read additional drivers from CD or USB drives like Vista can. When you're done, press Enter.

③ SELECT HARD DISKS
On the next screen, press Enter to install a fresh copy of Windows XP. Press F8 to accept the licence agreement. If you want to repair your installation, press R and skip to Step 5. For a new installation, select the partition on which you want Windows to be installed and go to Step 4.

If you have a new disk, select it (usually MB Disk 0). Press C to create a new partition. You have to select the partition size in megabytes (1,024MB equals 1GB). Generally, we'd recommend leaving at least 40GB (40,960MB) for the second partition, which you can use for backups and storing files you don't want to overwrite during a fresh operating system installation. Subtract the size of second partition you want from the figure in the box and enter this. Press Enter to apply. Select Unpartitioned Space and press C. Press Enter to create the partition. Don't worry if you've got a tiny amount of unpartitioned space left, as this space can't be used. Select C: and press Enter to install.

④ FORMAT HARD DISK
The installation routine has to format the hard disk before it can copy the Windows XP files

BEFORE YOU BEGIN:

A Repair installation won't fix every problem. If your computer's not working properly, it's best either to perform a fresh install of Windows XP using these instructions or restore a backup (see page 84).

If you're going to do a Repair installation, your Windows disc needs to contain the same version of service pack as your PC. If it doesn't, you'll need to create a slipstreamed disc (see http://tinyurl.com/slipstreamxp).

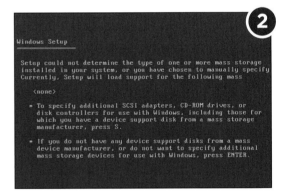

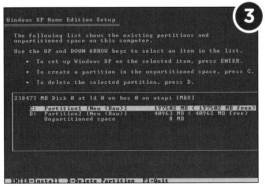

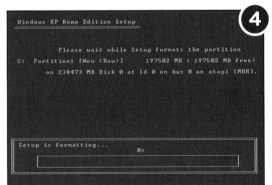

to it. Select Format NTFS and press Enter. While Vista has a speedy format option, XP's takes quite a while, and you may have to wait 30 minutes or more for it to complete.

Once the hard disk has been formatted, Windows files are copied to the disk. Your computer will reboot automatically once this is done and continue the installation using a graphical tool.

5 CHANGE REGIONAL SETTINGS

The first choice you get is to choose which language you want. Click Customize and change Standards and formats to United Kingdom. Change Location to United Kingdom, too. Click on the Languages tab and click on the Details button. Click Add, select United Kingdom as the input language and click OK.

Select US in the Installed services window and click Remove and then OK. You'll get a warning saying that it will be removed the next time you reboot your PC. Click OK on this message. Click on the Advanced tab and choose English (United Kingdom) from the drop-down menu. Click OK to apply these settings, then Next.

6 ENTER YOUR PRODUCT KEY

Enter your name in the next box, although you can leave the Organization field blank. Click Next. Enter your product key, which will be printed inside the box in which your copy of Windows XP came. On the next screen, give your PC a more meaningful name than the one that Windows gives it and click Next.

7 SET DATE AND TIME

Even though you told Windows in every setting that you're in the UK, it still sets itself to US time. Change the Time Zone option to GMT. Select the current date and time, and click Next.

Windows will next install the network drivers for your onboard network card. When prompted, leave the network setting as Typical settings and click Next. Windows will finish copying files and finalise the installation.

8 RUN WINDOWS FOR THE FIRST TIME

When Windows starts for the first time, click OK when the dialog box appears to tell you the screen resolution will be automatically changed. Click OK again to confirm that the new resolution

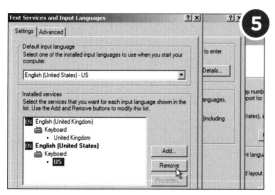

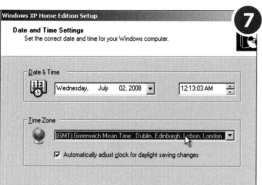

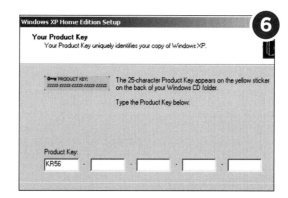

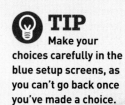

TIP
Make your choices carefully in the blue setup screens, as you can't go back once you've made a choice.

has worked. On the next screen, select 'Help protect my PC by turning on Automatic Updates now' and click Next. Enter your name on the next screen, and anyone else that will be using your computer (if you're doing a Repair installation make sure that you type in the same usernames as used originally and jump to Step 13). Click Next and then Finish. You can now remove the Windows XP installation CD.

9 INSTALL MOTHERBOARD DRIVERS
Although Windows is now working, you still need to install all the relevant drivers to make sure that everything will work smoothly. The first place to start is with the motherboard drivers. If you downloaded the drivers earlier, insert the USB key or disc you saved them to. If you can't do this, insert the provided driver disc and follow the onscreen instructions. Once you're connected to the internet, download the latest drivers (see page 10) and then follow these instructions.

For every driver you downloaded, run the associated file. It's best to start with the chipset driver, but the order afterwards doesn't matter. If Windows displays any warning messages, just click OK. Some files you download are just archive files that extract the real driver files to your hard disk. If this is the case, navigate to the folder the files were extracted to and run the Setup program you'll find there. You'll probably need to restart your PC after each driver installation.

10 INSTALL GRAPHICS CARD DRIVERS
Windows will install its own graphics drivers for any onboard or dedicated cards that you have. These are good enough to run Windows, but you won't be able to play games properly. Instead, you need to install the graphics drivers.

Both ATI and Nvidia provide a single driver package, so all you have to do is run the file you downloaded. If you couldn't download the drivers earlier, you need to insert the bundled CD, but remember to download newer drivers later on.

Restart your computer after the drivers have been installed. Right-click on the desktop, select Properties, then Settings, and change your display resolution to match your monitor's native resolution.

11 INSTALL OTHER PERIPHERALS
You can now install the other peripherals that you've added to your PC. Install the relevant driver files for each device that's plugged into your motherboard. For USB devices, you need to install the driver file first and, when prompted, connect the device to a USB port. If you're in any doubt, you should read the manual that came with your peripheral. If you've installed a wireless adaptor, make sure that you connect to your wireless network, following the provided instructions.

12 INSTALL SERVICE PACK 3
When everything is installed, you should install Windows XP Service Pack 3, unless the

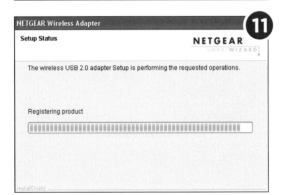

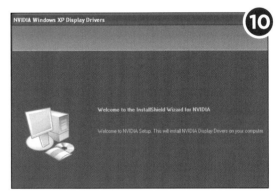

installation disc you used included it, in which case you can skip to the final step.

To install Service Pack 3, you should first connect to the internet. The easiest way to force it to install is to go to *http://tinyurl.com/ XPservicepack*. Click Download and save the file to your hard disk. When it's finished, run the file you downloaded. Follow the wizard through. Service Pack 3 will take up to an hour to install, restarting your computer when necessary.

⑬ RUN WINDOWS UPDATE

Visit *www.windowsupdate.com* and click on the Custom button. Windows Update will then prompt you to download the Windows Genuine Advantage Tool in order to use the service. Click the Download and Install Now button and follow the wizard through. Click Continue until you get back to the first screen and then click the Custom button again.

Windows Update will then search for the latest updates for your computer. When the list comes back, select the updates that you want, click Review and install updates, and then Install Updates to install them.

⑭ ACTIVATE WINDOWS

If your computer wasn't connected to the internet while you were installing Windows XP, it won't yet be activated. Windows XP puts a permanent icon in the Notification Area that displays regular messages warning you about activation. Double-click the icon that looks like two keys. In the next dialog box, select Yes, activate Windows over the internet now and click Next. Choose whether you want to register with Microsoft and click Next. You should get a message saying that you've activated Windows. Click OK. If not, you may need to activate it over the phone using the onscreen instructions.

⑮ USER SETTINGS

Your PC and its users are not password-protected by default. If you'd like to add some security to your PC, you can change this. Click on the Start menu and select the Control Panel. Click on User Accounts, select your user and click on Create a password. Enter your new password and click Create Password. On the next screen click Yes, Make Private to ensure your files and folders remain private. Repeat these steps for every user you want to be password-protected.

⑯ FORMAT HARD DISK

The Windows setup wizard only formats the disk partition on which Windows is installed. If you created a separate partition, you won't be able to use it yet, as it's not formatted. Click on the Start menu, My Computer, right-click the D: drive and select Format. Click OK, make sure that NTFS is selected and then click Format. You can now install your software on that partition. ⊙

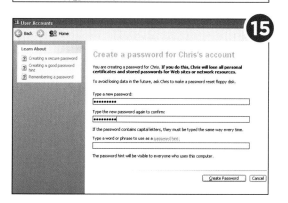

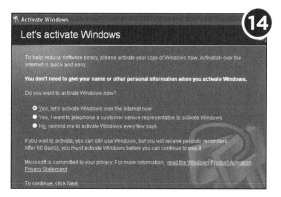

💡 TIP

It's essential that you run Windows Update after an installation to get the latest updates and security patches.

Chapter 10

Testing

MANY PROBLEMS CAN be quickly resolved with some diagnostic work. Here we'll show you how to look for and fix some common hardware problems. With the help of our essential diagnostic tools, you'll quickly be able to verify exactly what's wrong with your computer.

HOW TO...
Reset your CMOS

YOUR COMPUTER HOLDS all the settings about your PC's hardware in the CMOS. This includes information on the hard disks you have installed, the speed of your processor and the type and speed of memory you have.

When you install new hardware or encounter a problem, the information stored in the CMOS can become corrupted or out of date. Sometimes you may make a change to the hardware settings that means your computer won't start up. Fortunately, this is easy to fix by resetting the CMOS.

Before you start, turn off your computer. You'll need to open the side of it to gain access to the motherboard. It will also be helpful to have the motherboard's manual to hand.

① LOCATE CMOS RESET SWITCH
Your motherboard's manual will show you exactly where the CMOS reset switch is. If you don't have the manual, there are two options, depending on your computer: a jumper or a physical switch. A jumper is on your motherboard and will consist of two or three pins. It will probably have the words CMOS_RESET (or something similar) written next to it. A physical switch will usually be on the back of the motherboard where the keyboard, network and other devices plug in.

② RESET THE CMOS
For a jumper reset, take the jumper off its existing pins and cover the pin that was previously exposed and the pin next to it. For a button reset, push the button in and hold it in. You may need to use a pen to push it. Now press the power button, although your PC will not turn on. Instead, the CMOS will be cleared.

③ RESET BUTTON OR JUMPER
Once you've pushed the power button, your CMOS has been reset. Release the button if you have. If you're using a jumper, reset it to its original position. Press the power button on your PC again and this time it will spring to life. Depending on your PC, you may find that putting the jumper back in its original place powers the computer on. This is fine; just continue to Step 4.

④ CHANGE SETTINGS
When your PC turns on, press F1 to acknowledge that the CMOS has been reset. You'll automatically enter the computer's BIOS. You'll need to configure the BIOS (see page 102) to set up your computer properly. If you were making a change to the BIOS when your problems started, be careful not to make the same change again. ◯

TIP
A small number of PCs have a Reset CMOS button on the rear panel, so check for one before you open your computer.

Checking external cables

MANY PROBLEMS ARE caused by cables that either aren't plugged in or that have come loose. Before you start pulling your computer apart, you should check all the external cables to make sure that everything is connected properly. Here we'll explain all the ports on the back of your PC so that you can make sure that everything's plugged into the right place.

1 A PS/2 keyboard plugs into the round purple port

2 A PS/2 mouse plugs into the round green port

3 USB devices plug into these ports

4 Connect your speakers to these ports, matching the colour of the connector to the colour of the port (see page 48)

5 A VGA monitor should be plugged into your graphics card

6 A DVI-to-VGA adaptor allows you to plug a VGA cable into a digital output

7 A DVI monitor should be plugged into a graphics card's DVI output

8 The power cable plugs in here. Make sure the power switch on the power supply is turned on

Checking internal cables

YOUR POWER SUPPLY provides power for all your components. If the cables aren't connected properly or have come loose, you could end up with intermittent problems or a PC that simply doesn't work. Here we'll show you what the power supply's connectors do so you can make sure that they're connected properly. The information here will be useful throughout this chapter.

TIP
Tuck or tie any unwanted cables out of the way inside the case to improve airflow and keep your PC tidy.

1 The ATX connector provides power to your motherboard

2 The SATA connector is for hard disks and optical drives

3 A standard PCI Express graphics card connector

4 The newer 8-pin PCI-E power connector

5 The secondary motherboard power connector

6 A connector for floppy disks and memory card readers

7 The Molex connector is for hard disks

Motherboard connections

YOUR MOTHERBOARD IS is the centre of your computer, and all your components and peripherals plug directly into it. If any connectors or components aren't connected or have become loose, you can suffer from serious problems. This picture will help you locate where everything plugs in, which will make the guides later in this chapter easier to follow.

1 EXPANSION SLOTS These are used for internal peripherals such as TV tuners and graphics cards

2 PROCESSOR SOCKET For the processor

3 SECONDARY CONNECTOR The power supply's second connector plugs in here

4 USB/FIREWIRE HEADERS Extra USB or FireWire ports plug into these headers

5 SATA PORTS These are for hard disks, newer DVD writers and Blu-ray drives

6 FRONT PANEL CONNECTORS The power switch, reset switch and status light connect here

7 IDE PORT This is for attaching a DVD writer or an old hard disk

8 ATX CONNECTOR The power supply's ATX connector plugs in here

9 MEMORY SLOTS These are for your PC's memory

HOW TO...
Check internal cables

① POWER

To get your PC to turn on when you push the power button, you need to connect the power switch to the motherboard. Among the loose cables in your case, you'll find a two-pin connector. This will usually be marked PWR SW, but check the case's manual if you're not sure.

This needs to be connected to the power jumpers on the motherboard. Typically, these will be located on the bottom-right of the motherboard and will be marked, although you should double-check your motherboard's manual to make sure. The connector will plug on to the two pins and should connect easily.

② RESET

If your case has a reset switch – not all do – then there will be a similar connector to the power switch, with RESET SW written on it. Connecting this to your motherboard lets you restart your PC after a major crash, as it resets the hardware and forces your computer to reboot.

To connect it, you need to find the reset jumpers on the motherboard. These will be near the power switch, but you should read your motherboard's manual for the exact location. Simply push the connector over the two pins to connect the switch. It doesn't matter which way round this connector goes.

③ POWER AND HDD LEDs

The HDD connector connects to an LED on the front of the case and lights up when the hard disk is in operation. This is useful, as you can see whether your PC is working or if it's crashed.

As this connects to an LED, it must be connected correctly. The cable should be marked as positive and negative (usually written on the plug). The motherboard HDD jumper will also have a positive and negative port. Check your motherboard's manual carefully to make sure that you get this right, and then connect the cable.

Do the same thing for the power LED, which will have a similar connector. This must be connected the right way round, so make sure that you get the positive and negative connectors aligned.

④ USB

If your case has front-mounted USB ports or a card reader, you'll need to connect these to spare headers on your motherboard. In all likelihood, the cable in the case will be marked USB.

Your motherboard will probably have spare connectors marked USB, but the manual can tell

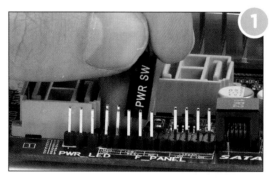

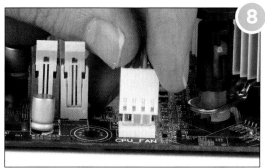

you exactly where these are. USB connectors take power, so you need to plug the cable in the right way round. Fortunately, the USB ports on most cases have a single plug that can be connected to the motherboard in only one way. If it doesn't, you'll need to check the case and motherboard manuals carefully to make sure that you install the connectors correctly.

Assuming you're using a block connector, plug it into a spare USB header on the motherboard. We'd recommend using the closest header to the cable to avoid draping cables everywhere.

5 FIREWIRE

Front-mounted FireWire cables plug in much the same way as USB cables. Again, look for a spare FireWire header on the motherboard (the manual will explain where these are) and connect the FireWire cable to it. The cable may be marked 1394, as FireWire is also known as i1394.

6 AUDIO

Front-mounted audio ports also need to be connected to the motherboard if you want to be able to plug in your headphones and a microphone. Fortunately, most motherboards and cases have a single block connector that plugs into the front audio connector on the motherboard.

Your motherboard's manual will have full details of where this is connected, but it's usually located by its back panel. Again, there's only one way to connect this cable, so just slide it gently into place. If your case has a Speaker header, plug this into

the appropriate connector on the motherboard. This is used to give warning beeps.

7 FANS

It's common for modern cases to have extra fans pre-fitted. These help increase airflow through the case and keep your PC cool. While fans can be connected directly to the power supply, it's better to connect them to spare fan headers on the motherboard. This way, the motherboard can automatically control the fan speed and keep your PC running as quietly as possible.

If your fans end in three- or four-pin connectors, you can plug them into your motherboard. Look at the manual to find a spare fan connector and then plug in the fan's power connector. Three-pin connectors can plug into four-pin ports and vice versa. These cables also only plug in one way, so it's easy to get it right.

8 CPU FAN

The processor fan has to be connected to the motherboard. In the same way as system fans, the processor's fan speed is controlled by the motherboard based on the processor's temperature. This keeps your computer as quiet as possible.

There's a special connector for the processor fan on the motherboard, which is often called CPU Fan. Check your motherboard's manual for its location. This is likely to be a four-pin connector, but three-pin processor fans can also be used. The connector can only go in one way.

TIP
LED connectors need to be connected the right way round, or they won't work.

Testing memory

MEMORY IS ONE of the most important components in your PC. It stores every aspect of the programs and data that you're currently running, from the window showing your holiday snaps to the spreadsheet with your accounts. Memory also holds important Windows data, such as device driver information and the core components of how Windows works.

A problem with memory can, therefore, be incredibly serious. For example, if your memory should corrupt a critical part of Windows, when the processor tries to use this data it can end up causing a serious system crash. This can result in damage to Windows and the loss of important data that you may have been working on.

To prevent this happening, it's worth running some diagnostic tests on your computer using the free Memtest86+ (*www.memtest.org*). This utility runs directly from a bootable CD before Windows has started and performs a series of tests on your system memory. Any problems reported here could lead to major problems in Windows. The step-by-step guide opposite shows you how to run the test, but here we'll explain what to do with the results.

ERRORS

An error doesn't automatically mean that you have a major problem with your memory. First, try checking the BIOS to find out what speed your memory is running at (see page 102 for instructions on how to do this). If it's running faster than it's supposed to, then you could be pushing it too much. Our guide on testing for system heat

on page 138 is also worth checking. If your system's temperature is too high, then your PC could be suffering from its effects.

It's always worth checking the obvious things, too. If you didn't plug your memory all the way in, it may be detected but cause intermittent faults. Try unplugging your memory and reseating it. Once you've done this try, run the Memtest86+ program again to see if the problem has disappeared. If it hasn't, it's time to try a new tack.

SWITCH SLOTS

It could be that one of the memory slots is causing the problem. Try switching memory slots on your motherboard and rerunning the test. If you're getting the same error, there's probably something wrong with your memory. You can attempt to find out which stick of RAM is causing the problems by taking out all the memory bar one stick and running the tests again. By rotating the stick of installed memory, you'll be able to track down the offending module.

As processors access memory through their own onboard caches, your processor could be causing the error. If you change your memory and the problem persists, you should change the processor or motherboard.

TIP

Often, only one stick of memory is at fault, so it's worth replacing each stick one by one to try and solve any problems.

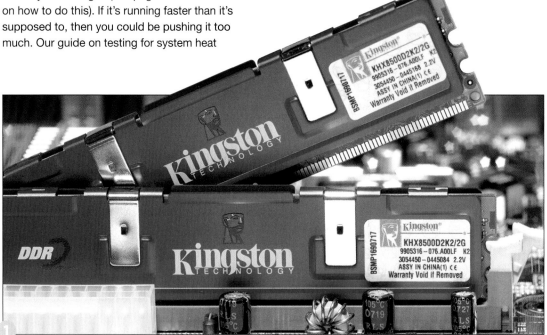

1 A problem with your system memory can make your PC frustrating to use

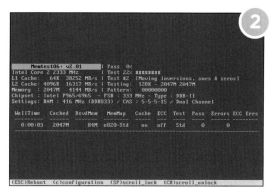

HOW TO...
Test your memory

1 CREATE BOOT DISK

Memtest86+ runs from a CD. Download the ISO file from *www.memtest.org* and save it to your hard disk. If you already have a CD-burning utility such as CDBurnerXP, you can follow the instructions for writing the ISO file to CD. If you haven't, download the free ISO Recorder from *http://isorecorder.alexfeinman.com*. Version 2 is for Windows XP and Version 3 is for Vista, so make sure you get the right one.

Once the software's installed, find the ISO file you downloaded, right-click on it and select Copy image to CD. Put a blank disc in your optical drive and click Next.

2 BOOT FROM THE CD

Put the CD that you just created into your drive and restart the computer. Make sure that your BIOS is set to boot from the optical drive. The CD will automatically load the test environment and start running the tests.

On the screen, you'll see system information and the current test status. The test can take 20 minutes or more to run, so you should leave it running. When it finishes, you'll either get details of

the errors discovered or a message saying that your memory has passed the test.

3 COMPARE DATA

The details on the screen show you the speed at which your memory is running. This is displayed after the settings heading, in brackets after DDR. You should compare this to the speed at which it's supposed to be running. If the detected speed is faster than the memory's rated speed, you could have a problem. However, don't worry about small fluctuations in speed, such as a difference of around five per cent. It's common for the timings to be slightly wrong and components made to run a bit quicker than their rated speeds.

4 CONFIGURE TEST

If you want to configure which test to run, you need to press C while the initial test is running. You may need to reset your computer and boot from the CD you created to get this option. In the menu, press 1 to access the test selection. Press 3 to select the test you want to run, and then type a number from 0 to 9 to run that test. You can find a list of the tests on the Memtest website.

Testing your hard disk

WE'VE ALL BECOME used to having masses of storage space, which most of us stuff full of gigabytes of photos, videos, music and important documents without a second thought. As wonderful as this all is, hard disks are mechanical and therefore quite sensitive. They can fail rapidly and, even if they don't lock up completely, they can cause problems with some files.

Although you should make regular backups of your data, it's also worth checking your hard disk if you're suffering from problems to make sure that it's working properly. Don't worry if you find a problem, as you can use the guide on taking an image of your PC (see page 84) to save your installed operating system and restore this to a new hard disk.

We'll show you how to test your hard disk for free using Hitachi GST's Drive Fitness Test application (*www.hitachigst.com/hdd/support/download.htm*). Although it's made by Hitachi, it works on all brands of hard disks. It's run from a bootable CD, which we'll show you how to make.

HOW HARD DISKS WORK

The problem with hard disks is that they're mechanical, and are therefore prone to faults. Inside the sealed enclosure are a series of platters, which are disks stacked above each other. These platters, like floppy disks, store data magnetically, and are written to and read by heads that sit just above the surface. Hard disks are therefore very sensitive to movements, as sudden jerks can make the heads touch the platter and destroy any data that's stored on the disk.

If you get problems when you run Drive Fitness Test, make sure your hard disk is firmly attached inside the case and that your computer is standing on a level surface. We've known of a computer that was kept on an old wobbly desk constantly having problems with corrupted Windows files.

PROBLEM DETECTION

Other problems can affect a disk, including lots of bad areas on the disk (known as sectors). These might be detected in normal use only when you fill your disk up and your computer starts trying to access these areas. By running a system scan beforehand, you can detect these bad sectors

now. These will be marked as bad by the hard disk, which prevents data being written to them, but you should replace the hard disk if you find that you get a large number of bad sectors.

Mechanical problems are also a big worry. A damaged disk can make a horrible, metallic clunking sound. While there's little that can be done to prevent this in the long term, running diagnostic tests that access the whole disk can warn you of potential mechanical failure in the future by giving the hard disk a good workout.

Heat, as for other components, can cause massive problems inside a hard disk, so make sure that the inside of your PC is kept cool, and add more cooling if necessary (see page 132 for more information).

Modern hard disks have built-in S.M.A.R.T. technology. This lets your BIOS and other applications talk to the disk and see if there are any problems. S.M.A.R.T. can also notify you of an impending disk failure before it happens.

Finally, the interface between the hard disk and your PC can cause problems if it's damaged. In this case, there's nothing you can do but replace the hard disk. It's worth checking that the cables are plugged in firmly first, though.

1 Hard disks are mechanical devices that can malfunction in a number of ways

HOW TO...
Test your hard disk

1 CREATE BOOT DISC

Drive Fitness Test runs from a CD that you can create yourself. Download the ISO file from *www.hitachigst.com/hdd/support/download.htm* and save it to your hard disk. If you already have a CD-burning utility, you can use that to write the ISO file to CD.

If you don't have a CD-burning application, download the free ISO Recorder from *http://isorecorder.alexfeinman.com*. Version 2 is for Windows XP and Version 3 is for Windows Vista, so make sure you get the right one. Once the software's installed, right-click on the ISO file you downloaded and select Copy image to CD. Put a blank CD into your optical drive and click Next.

2 BOOT FROM THE CD

Put the CD in your optical drive and restart your PC. Set the BIOS so that your optical drive is the first boot device (see page 102). You'll be given a menu with a choice of two options. Select the second option, press Enter and accept the licence agreement. The Drive Fitness Test program will then detect your hard disks, and ask for confirmation that this list is correct. Select Yes.

3 RUN A QUICK TEST

Select the hard disk that you want to test and then choose Quick Test. On the next screen, click Start. Drive Fitness Test will now run a series of diagnostic tests on your hard disk to make sure it's working properly. If the software detects any errors, you'll be told at the end of the test; otherwise, you'll get a green completion message. Click OK to accept it.

With a brand new disk this should be good enough to show that it's working correctly. If you're testing a hard disk from an old computer, follow Step 4 for a more in-depth test.

4 ADVANCED TEST

The Quick Test doesn't give the drive a full workout. For this you need to run the Advanced Test. This will run more thorough tests and check the surface of the disk for errors.

As this involves checking every part of the disk, this test will take a lot longer to run than the Quick Test, but it's worth doing, particularly if you're checking an old hard disk. It's also essential if you think that your hard disk could be causing problems.

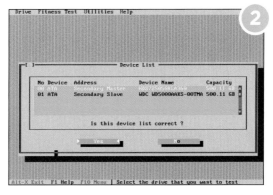

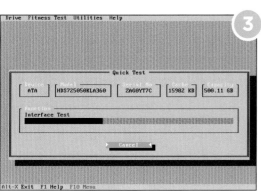

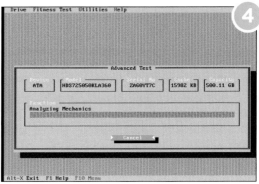

TIP
You should run Windows Check Disk on your hard disks regularly to find and fix faults before they become too serious.

Testing your PC for heat

EVERYTHING INSIDE YOUR computer generates heat to some degree. It may seem obvious that your processor does – after all, it has a giant fan and heatsink on top of it – but all components produce a certain amount of heat. Memory, hard disks, graphics cards and even your optical drive all contribute to the overall internal temperature of your PC's case.

Heat is a big problem inside computers. If your PC is too hot, you'll find that it will crash more often, as the components shut themselves down to prevent damage. In the long term, the effects of too much heat inside your system can cause your components to have a shorter lifespan. In the case of your hard disk, this could see it failing before its time, taking some of your important data with it.

MONITOR AND MEASURE

It's really important, therefore, to make sure that your PC is running at the right temperature. Keeping it cool will save you trouble and hassle further down the line. Our step-by-step guide on the opposite page shows you how to monitor your computer's temperature with the free utility SpeedFan. You can download this from *www. almico.com/speedfan.php*.

Click the download tab and click the link in the download section of the page. Once installed, it can monitor and help control the temperature inside your PC. Before you can set it properly, though, you need to know what should be expected from your system.

IDEAL TEMPERATURES

To get SpeedFan working properly, you'll have to set some maximum temperatures. These can be tricky to work out, but we've got some tips that should help. Hard disks, for example, shouldn't run any higher than 55°C, or they can be damaged. Overall system temperature inside the case should be kept below 50°C, but the lower the better.

Processors are harder to measure, as it depends on the type of chip that you're using. Generally speaking, AMD processors should have an external temperature of less than 40°C. Intel processors should have an external temperature of less than 55°C.

You may find that, depending on your system, your temperatures are either close to these figures or a lot lower. Much depends on the temperature sensors in your PC. Motherboard manufacturers use different types of sensors in different locations, which can cause a lot of variance between boards. As long as you're running your PC at temperatures less than we've highlighted, though, it will be fine.

MORE FANS

If your PC is running really hot, there are some things you can try to lower the temperature. First, reseat your processor cooler, making sure it has enough thermal paste on it to increase the efficiency of the heatsink. Make sure your case's fans aren't clogged up with dust. If you can control your fans manually, try turning them up.

Finally, if you haven't got any case fans or have enough space for more, then install some. They're easy to fit, and pretty much every case has mountings for them. Inspect your case's manual for full instructions on the size of fans you can install. Ideally, you want to get airflow moving through the case to extract hot air. So, if your fan at the rear is blowing out the back of the case, fit one in the front that blows into the case. This will bring in cool air from outside and help push the hot air out of the case. If you have one hot component, such as a hard disk, then you need to fit fans near it to help cool it down.

💡 **TIP**
Fans have arrows printed on them showing the direction of the airflow.

❶ **Keeping your PC cool will help extend its lifespan**

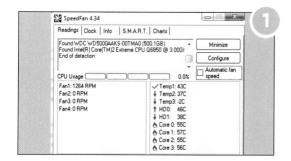

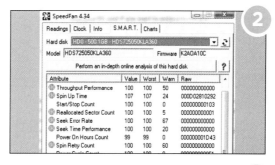

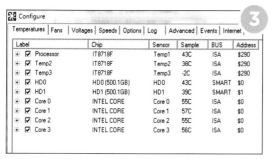

HOW TO...
Monitor system temperature

1 READINGS

SpeedFan automatically detects temperature sensors on the motherboard and displays their current readings. Unfortunately, it doesn't always give them recognisable names, so it can be hard to tell which one is your processor's temperature and which one is the system temperature. The easiest way to find out is to leave your system idle for a few minutes until the temperatures settle. Note down the temperatures, restart your computer and go into the BIOS. Its monitoring section will give you real names for the sensors – all you have to do is match the relative values you recorded.

SpeedFan places an icon next to each temperature reading, which is designed to show you the current status of your computer. A green tick means that everything's all right, arrows show whether the temperature is increasing or decreasing, while a fire means that it's too hot. However, SpeedFan doesn't always get the warnings right, so ignore them for now.

2 HDD AND CORE

As well as accessing the motherboard, SpeedFan can read the temperature of your hard disks using Self-Monitoring Analysis and Reporting Technology (S.M.A.R.T.). Each disk in your PC will be numbered (HD0, HD1 and so on) and have its own temperature. You can also get a report on

your hard disk by clicking on the S.M.A.R.T. tab. The core temperatures are the readings from inside your processor.

3 CONFIGURE SETTINGS

Click on the Readings tab and then on Configure. You'll see the list of temperature sensors. Click to select one, wait a few seconds and then click again. You can now rename the sensor to match what you identified in Step 1. Press Enter to set the name.

Click on a sensor and you'll see two readings: desired and warning. The first is an ideal temperature, while warning determines when a flame will be displayed. You only need to set the warning temperatures for hard disks and the processor, as defined by the limits opposite.

4 CHARTS

Click on the Charts tab and put ticks in the sensors that you want to measure. SpeedFan will then track temperatures over time. This is a good way to see how your system responds when you do different jobs. For example, if you play a lot of games and see that your PC's temperature is running very high during this activity, you'll know that you need to get some extra cooling. This can also be useful when running burn-in tests, such as Hot CPU Tester (see page 134).

Testing your processor

THE PROCESSOR IS just about the most important part of your PC. Without it, you'd just have a collection of components that wouldn't be able to do anything. The processor controls every single aspect of your computer, from loading and running the operating system to running the clever artificial intelligence in the latest games.

Processors are constantly being updated, and are also becoming more complicated. These days, it's the norm for a single chip to house at least two processors (called cores), but four cores are rapidly becoming more affordable. While this extra complexity means that computers today can storm through tough tasks such as video encoding quicker than ever, the result is that there's more that can go wrong.

A processor crashing will immediately freeze your computer, losing any unsaved work in the process. If the hard disk was being accessed at the time with an important Windows system file open, a processor crash can even mean that you need to reinstall Windows. Here we'll show you how to test your computer for stability with the free Hot CPU Tester (available from *www.7byte.com*).

PROBLEM SOLVING

The free version of Hot CPU Tester doesn't run the full suite of diagnostics, which is available in the Professional version. However, there's enough there to make sure that your processor is running properly. Using its Burn-in test, you can find out how effective your processor's cooling is.

The most common reason for a processor to fail any of the diagnostic tests is overheating. Processors are sensitive to heat, and can start causing errors when they get too hot. Intel's processors try to deal with the problem by slowing themselves down, which makes your computer very sluggish until the core temperature has dropped. Alternatively, processors can shut themselves down completely, meaning that you'll need to restart your computer.

COOLING OFF

The essential thing with processors is to make sure that there's plenty of cooling. Follow our step-by-step advice opposite to work out how hot your processor is. If it exceeds the limits we set on page 132, you've got a problem. Take your PC apart and make sure that its fan is working and that there's decent contact between the processor and the cooler. You may need to reapply thermal paste.

If heat doesn't seem to be the problem and your processor is still failing diagnostic checks, make sure you're running it at the intended speed in the BIOS (see page 102). Running the processor faster than it is meant to can cause errors.

Finally, try taking the processor out of its socket (see pages 136 and 137 for full instructions). In Intel LGA-775 sockets, look for any bent pins. If you see any, push them gently back into place with a jeweller's screwdriver. For AM2 and AM2+ processors, make sure that you haven't bent any pins on the processor. Inserting a credit card between the rows should allow you to bend them back into shape. Take great care when doing this or you could cause more damage.

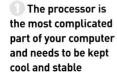
The processor is the most complicated part of your computer and needs to be kept cool and stable

HOW TO...
Test your processor

1 SET THE TEST DURATION

Install Hot CPU Tester (*www.7byte.com*) and run it when the installation has finished. Click OK to skip the message about upgrading to the new version. Before you start, click on the Options tab and select the Test Modules item. You'll see that the test duration is set to six hours. While this will give your PC a thorough workout, it's probably too much for most people. We'd recommend setting it to an hour or slightly under.

2 RUN TEST

Click on the Diagnostic button and click Run Test. Hot CPU Tester will then give your processor a thorough workout. It will run lots of mathematically complex tasks to stretch your processor to its limit. It will use every core in your PC, so you'll be unable to use your computer for anything else during this time.

Once the program has finished the test, you'll receive a report telling you if your processor failed any of the tests. If it didn't, you know that it's working properly.

3 BURN IN

Click the Burn-in icon. This test will run your processor at 100 per cent load, and is useful for checking how temperature affects it. However, in the free version of Hot CPU Tester, which tests only a single core, you can run only a single thread. A workaround is to run Hot CPU Tester as many times as you have cores by double-clicking the program icon.

4 MEASURE

Before you start the Burn-in test, run SpeedFan (see page 133) in order to measure the temperature. Keep it somewhere onscreen where it will be visible. Start the Burn-in test on every open copy of Hot CPU Tester by clicking the Run CPU Burn-in button. SpeedFan may stop responding, as your processor is too busy to deal with it. Don't worry; just leave the test running for around 10 minutes and then stop all the Burn-in tests. When they've stopped, look at the temperature of the processor in SpeedFan. If it's exceeded the limits you set for it, you may have overheating problems.

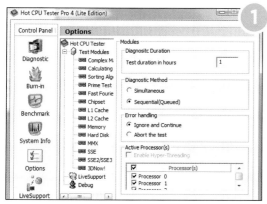

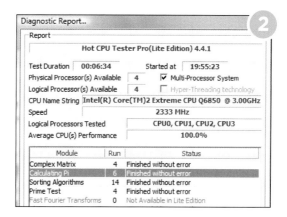

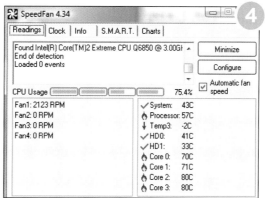

TIP

If you have fan speed switches on or inside your case, try using them to increase fan speed to cool down a hot processor.

HOW TO...
Reseat an Intel processor

INTEL PROCESSORS DON'T have any pins on them; instead, the socket is made up of lots of delicate connectors, so make sure you don't damage them when you're touching the processor.

1 REMOVE THE FAN AND PROCESSOR

First, turn the feet on the cooler in the direction of the arrow, then pull them up sharply and remove the cooler. Unplug its power cable from the motherboard.

To access the processor, unclip the handle that runs down the side of the socket and lift it up. Lift the cage up and out of the way to expose the socket. Grip the processor around its edges and lift it slowly up and out of the way.

2 REPLACE THE PROCESSOR

Your processor has two cut-out notches in its sides, which line up with the ridges in the socket. This prevents it from being inserted the wrong way round. You'll also notice an arrow on the processor. This should line up with the corner of the socket that has its pins arranged diagonally.

Line up the processor as described above, and put it gently in place. If it doesn't fit properly, then you've got it the wrong way round. Once you're happy the processor is in place, close the cage and pull the retaining handle down. This should take a bit of force, but if it feels like there's too much resistance, check that the processor is seated properly.

3 TOP UP THERMAL PASTE

Thermal paste fills in any space between the surface of the processor and the surface of the cooler, ensuring that there's efficient heat transfer between the two. You'll need to clean off any existing paste and apply some more (a tube costs around £5). Take the tube and squeeze a tiny blob into the middle of the processor. Use a small piece of card to spread the paste thinly until the processor's surface is coated.

4 CONNECT THE FAN

Take the fan you removed and turn its feet away from the direction of the arrows. Line up the cooler so that the four feet touch the holes in the motherboard. Starting at diagonally opposite sides, push the four feet into the place. You'll need to use some force, and the feet should click into position. Finally, check that the cooler is seated properly and that it isn't wobbly. If it is, check that the feet are properly in position. Plug its power connector into the motherboard header marked CPU.

💡 TIP
The plastic clips on Intel coolers can be awkward to fit. Make sure the black plastic clips are raised before fitting the cooler, and push diagonally opposite clips in together.

HOW TO...
Reseat an AMD processor

AMD PROCESSORS HAVE delicate pins on the underside. Remove and insert the processor squarely to prevent damage.

1 REMOVE THE FAN AND PROCESSOR

Push down the handle on the cooler and move it around the retaining clip. The handle will lift up, allowing you to slip the retaining mount off the plastic clips. Pick the cooler up gently, and tilt it towards the remaining clip holding it in place. If it feels stuck, slide it from side to side until it loosens. Once you've lifted it, unplug its power connector.

Unclip the handle on the processor socket and lift it up. Hold the processor by its sides and lift it vertically out of the way.

2 PUT THE PROCESSOR BACK

The processor can only fit one way into the socket. Make sure that the arrow on top of the processor is aligned with the gold arrow on the socket. Gently push the processor into place. You should feel it click into position when it's all the way in. If you have to use too much force, stop and check that the processor is correctly aligned.

Once the processor is all the way in, check around it to make sure that it's sitting flush against the plastic socket. If it's not, push gently down on the corners that aren't flush. Push the lever down and clip it back into place to secure the processor.

3 TOP UP THERMAL PASTE

Thermal paste fills in any space between the surface of the processor and the surface of the cooler, ensuring that there's efficient heat transfer between the two. You'll need to clean off any existing paste and apply some more.

Tubes of thermal paste cost around £5. Take the tube and squeeze a tiny blob into the middle of the processor. Use a small piece of card to spread the paste around thinly, so that the surface of the processor is coated.

4 CONNECT THE FAN

Around the processor socket is a plastic cooler mount, with two nodules sticking out. These are designed to hold the cooler's clips.

Take your cooler and open its handle. Fit the metal clip without the handle on it over one nodule and push it snugly against the mount. Place the cooler flat on top of the surface of the processor.

Push the cooler's remaining metal clip over the second nodule and close the handle. This will require quite a bit of force to get the handle all the way down. Plug the fan's power connector back into the motherboard header marked CPU.

TIP
If the pins on an AMD processor are bent, a credit card can be slid between the rows of bent pins to straighten them.

HOW TO...
Reseat PC memory

MEMORY CAN BECOME faulty, so try putting the memory back one stick at a time. If you have spare slots, try these if you're still having problems. Pairs of memory modules need to be installed in in the correct slots, so check your motherboard's manual for the correct configuration or replace the memory in the slots in which it was originally installed.

① REMOVE MEMORY
Open the white plastic clips on either side of the memory module. This will free the memory from the socket. Grab the stick at either end and pull it upwards to remove it.

Do the same for any other memory modules that are installed.

② REFIT MEMORY
To refit the memory, you need to slide it into the slot. Make sure that the notch in the memory lines up with the ridge in the socket. If it doesn't, then the memory is the wrong way round.

Push firmly on both sides of the memory module to push it into place. The clips should spring back up and click into position. Check the clips are in place and nestled against the notches in the side of the memory module. If they're not, try pushing the memory down a bit further. You can also push the clips up to help them lock into place. Repeat this for any remaining modules.

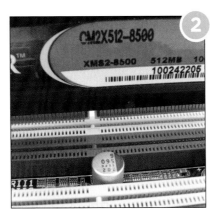

HOW TO...
Reseat laptop memory

LAPTOP MEMORY IS usually harder to reach than desktop PC memory. Opening your laptop can also invalidate the warranty, so take special care.

① REMOVE MEMORY
First, you need to open up your laptop to get at the memory sockets. There will typically be a door underneath the laptop that gives you easy access – you'll simply have to unscrew it and lift it out of the way.

If your memory is located under your laptop's keyboard, you'll need to remove this first. Your laptop's manual may explain how to do this; otherwise you'll have to work it out yourself. Look for any clips or retaining screws. Be careful, as keyboards are delicate and can have short cables that are easily disconnected.

When you've found the memory slots, push the two metal clips aside and the memory module will spring up. Simply pull it out.

② FIT MEMORY
Align the notch in the memory module with the notch in the slot. Slide the memory into place until its connector is completely covered. Push it down gently and the retaining metal clips will click into place and hold the memory firmly in place.

Reseating a hard disk

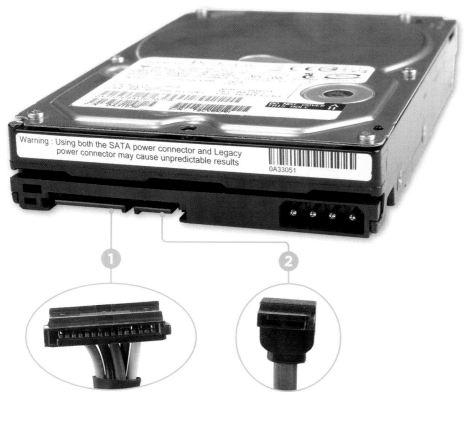

① SATA POWER
Remove and reconnect the hard disk's power supply here.

② SATA DATA Remove and reconnect one end of the data cable in here and the other end into a SATA port on the motherboard.

③ IDE CONNECTOR Remove and reconnect the IDE data cable in here. The red cable on the IDE connector should be closest to the power connector.

④ JUMPER Use this to set the drive to master or slave.

⑤ THE POWER CONNECTOR Remove and reconnect a Molex power connector here.

 **LAPTOP TIP**

Laptop hard disks are usually mounted in cages, which may or may not be easily accessible. Look for a symbol of three stacked circles on the bottom of your laptop to identify which screws to remove.

Reseating an optical drive

1 SATA POWER
Remove and reconnect the optical drive's power here.

2 SATA DATA Remove and reconnect one end of the data cable in here and the other end into a SATA port on the motherboard.

3 IDE CONNECTOR Remove and reconnect the IDE data cable in here. The red cable on the IDE connector should be closest to the power connector.

4 JUMPER Use this to set the drive to master or slave.

5 THE POWER CONNECTOR Remove and reconnect a Molex power connector here.

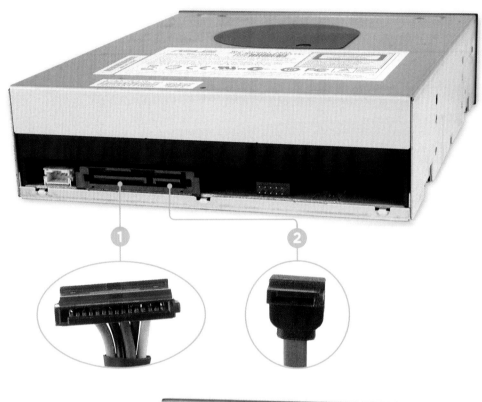

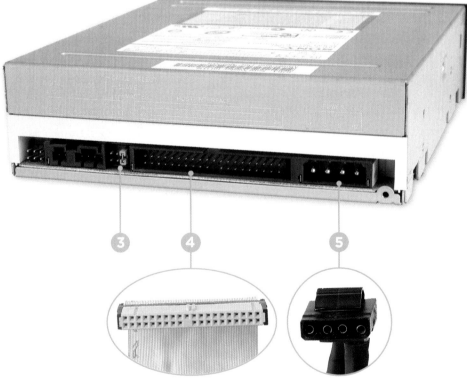

Laptop optical drives sometimes have quick-release mechanisms, but may also have one or two screws securing them in place underneath the laptop.

HOW TO...
Reseat expansion cards

ALL EXPANSION CARDS are connected in roughly the same way, but watch out for any additional power cables. If your cards are all grouped together in consecutive slots, it's worth taking the time to space them out to reduce heat.

1 REMOVE THE GRAPHICS CARD
Unscrew the blanking plate or, if your case has no screws, unclip the retaining bracket. Unplug the monitor cables plugged into the graphics card. Your card will have a retaining clip at the back of the PCI Express x16 slot. These either push down or away from the graphics card and release the card. Once the clip has been depressed, pull the graphics card firmly out of the way.

2 REFIT THE GRAPHICS CARD
Line up the graphics card's connector with the slot in the case. The card should look as if it's pointing down, with the fan pointing towards the bottom of the case. Pressure on both ends of the card should be enough to make sure that it ends up seated in the expansion card slot properly. You should check the card when you think it's in place to ensure that you've made proper contact. If you can still see some of the card's slot sticking out, push the offending slide in a bit further.

Screw the blanking plate back in or reattach the retaining bracket. Reconnect your monitor cables.

3 REMOVE EXPANSION CARDS
Unscrew the blanking plate or, if your case has no screws, unclip the retaining bracket. Unplug any cables plugged into the expansion card. There are no retaining clips, so grip the card firmly at both ends and pull it straight back.

4 REFIT EXPANSION CARDS
Line up the card's connector with the slot in the case. The card should have the notches in its connector lined up with the notches in the slot. Pressure on both ends of the card should be enough to make sure that it ends up seated in the expansion card slot properly.

Check the card when you think it's in place to ensure that you've made proper contact. If you can still see some of the card's slot sticking out, push the protruding part in a bit further. Screw the blanking plate back in or reattach the retaining bracket, and finally reconnect any cables.

Glossary

From ADSL to ZIF, we explain 100 key PC terms – with pictures

10/100Mbit/s See Ethernet.

10BASE-T See Ethernet.

64-BIT 64-bit processors have an extended instruction set, allowing them to process more data at once and access more memory. Only software that supports 64-bit extensions will benefit.

802.11b, 802.11g See WiFi.

ADSL Asymmetric digital subscriber line, the commonest form of broadband. It works over existing BT phone lines, provided that the local exchange is ADSL-enabled.

AGP Accelerated graphics port, a slot for graphics cards. Several versions of increasing speed and decreasing voltage were launched. Now superseded by PCI Express.

ATA AT attachment. See IDE.

ATAPI AT attachment packet interface. See IDE.

ATHLON 64 AMD's current mainstream processor. Has been made for Socket 754, Socket 939 and now Socket AM2.

ATX POWER CONNECTOR This PSU connector supplies the PC's motherboard. It was previously a 20-pin connector, but a 24-pin version started appearing on motherboards in 2005. A split connector is commonly provided to power either version.

ATX See Form Factor.

BIOS The basic input/output system configures your motherboard at startup and boots your PC. It's stored on a flash memory chip and keeps its settings in the CMOS.

BLANKING PLATE Used to cover unoccupied PC case cutouts. You must remove one to install a PCI, PCI Express or AGP expansion card.

BTX See Form Factor.

CARDBUS The 32-bit expansion slot most commonly found on laptop PCs, equivalent to the PCI slot on desktops. Is now being superseded by ExpressCard.

CAT5, CAT6 See Ethernet.

CELERON Intel's budget processor. Current models are cut-down Pentium 4s, available for Socket 478 and LGA775.

CLOCK SPEED All computer components work in time with a clock signal. Each has a maximum speed, shown in megahertz (MHz) or gigahertz (GHz), at which it's designed to run. Running the clock faster (overclocking) boosts performance, but can cause a PC to crash.

CMOS Battery-backed memory where the BIOS stores its settings. Can be cleared using a jumper.

COMPONENT VIDEO A high-quality analogue video connection using three cables.

COMPOSITE VIDEO A basic-quality video connection using a single cable.

CORE 2 Intel's most common processor, available for LGA775 in mainstream Duo and Quad and premium Extreme versions.

CORE i7 Intel's newest processor has a completely new architecture and works in LGA1366 motherboards only.

CPU Central processing unit, also known simply as a processor.

CROSSFIRE ATI's system for combining the power of two Radeon graphics cards in a single PC. Also see SLI.

CRT Cathode ray tube. Refers to a conventional glass-tube monitor.

DDR The type of memory used in many PCs, called double data rate because it runs twice as fast as its clock speed. Comes in several speeds, including PC2700 and PC3200. PC3200 DDR runs at 200MHz but is called 400MHz DDR because of its doubled effective speed.

DDR2 The type of memory used in the majority of Pentium 4, Core 2, Athlon 64 and Phenom systems. Available in speeds from PC2-4200 (533MHz effective).

DDR3 The type of memory used by newer Core i7 and Phenom systems. It's available in speeds from PC3-6400 (800MHz), up to PC3-12800 (1,600MHz).

DHCP Dynamic host configuration protocol. This allows PCs on a network to obtain their network configuration automatically from a DHCP server.

DIRECTX Windows extensions from Microsoft that give games and other performance-hungry software fast access to hardware. Check that your PC has the latest version – currently 10 – installed.

DRAFT-N A term used for wireless networking equipment based on the draft 802.11n standard.

D-SUB Analogue monitor-to-graphics-card connection, also known as a VGA cable.

DUAL-CHANNEL Capability of a processor or motherboard to access two DIMMs at once, improving performance.

DVB-T Digital Video Broadcasting – Terrestrial, a standard used by Freeview digital TV in the UK.

DVI Digital visual interface. A monitor-to-graphics-card connection that can include digital and/or analogue signals. The commonest form, DVI-I, has both.

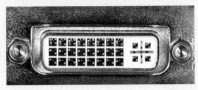

ETHERNET Non-specific networking term, today used to refer to any networking hardware using RJ45 plugs and one of a number of compatible standards including 10BaseT, 100BaseT and Gigabit Ethernet (GbE). Older 10/100Mbit/s hardware supports the two slower speeds, and runs reliably with the Category 5 (Cat5) grade of cable. Cat5e cables are needed for Gigabit.

EXPRESSCARD Expansion slot found on new laptop PCs, equivalent to PCI Express on desktops. Incompatible with CardBus.

FAT32 See NTFS.

FIREWALL Software or hardware designed to protect networks from hackers or from software that they control.

FIREWIRE Also known as IEEE 1394 or i.Link. Fast data connection used by PCs, digital camcorders, external hard disks and more. The connector comes in four-pin and six-pin versions, the latter including pins to power one device from the other. A faster nine-pin version, known as FireWire 800, is backward-compatible.

FIRMWARE Software used by a hardware device and stored on a flash memory chip so that it can be upgraded, typically to improve compatibility.

FLASH A type of memory chip that stores data permanently unless it is deliberately overwritten, a process known as flashing.

FLOPPY POWER CONNECTOR
A compact four-pin power connector for floppy drives.

FORM FACTOR Motherboards adhere to standards called form factors that dictate size and layout. The commonest are ATX and its compact relative microATX. BTX is Intel's newest standard. Cases will support one or more form factors, telling you which motherboards can be fitted.

FSB The frontside bus connects the processor and other parts of the system. On all but the latest motherboards, the memory runs at the same speed as the FSB – typically 133MHz, 200MHz or 266MHz.

GIGABIT ETHERNET (GbE) See Ethernet.

HEADER
A group of pins on a motherboard where you can connect additional ports. USB and FireWire headers are the most common.

IDE A common name for the ATA disk connector, strictly called ATAPI in its modern form, which supports a variety of devices. All three are also known as PATA (Parallel ATA), to distinguish them from SATA (Serial ATA).

IEEE 1394 See FireWire.

JUMPER A plastic-enclosed metal contact used to connect two pins to configure a hardware device. For example, see Master.

LGA775 Intel's current processor socket, with pins rather than holes. Used by Pentium 4, Celeron and Core 2 processors.

LGA1366 Intel's current processor socket. An update to LGA775, designed for use with the Core i7 processors.

LINE-IN Audio input for signal of standard 'line-level' volume (louder than microphone input). Usually light blue and takes a 3.5mm jack.

LINE-OUT Audio output of standard 'line-level' volume. Usually lime green, and takes a 3.5mm jack.

MASTER
Two IDE devices can share a single cable, provided that one is configured as a master and the other as a slave. This is done using jumpers on the devices.

MICROATX A compact mainstream motherboard form factor of maximum size 244x244mm.

MIMO Multiple-input, multiple-output: a way of improving the range and performance of wireless (WiFi) networks using multi-faceted antennas. A technology, not a standard. See Pre-N.

MOLEX Common name for the four-pin power connector used by hard disks and other drives. It has yellow (12V), red (5V) and two black (ground) wires.

NTFS Hard disk file system used by XP, Vista and other advanced versions of Windows. Replaces FAT32, as used by Windows 95, 98 and Me.

OEM Original equipment manufacturer. Used to describe products intended for PC manufacturers rather than end users. Typically these will have minimal packaging and manuals.

PATA See IDE.

PC100, PC133 See SDRAM.

PC1600, PC2100, PC2700, PC3200 See DDR.

PC2-4200 See DDR2.

PCI A motherboard expansion slot used for all kinds of upgrade cards except graphics cards. Internal modems, TV tuners and sound cards generally use PCI.

PCI EXPRESS (PCI-E) New expansion bus for all kinds of upgrades. Slots come in several lengths. Long, fast x16 slots are for graphics cards; short, slower x1 slots are for devices previously made for PCI. A slower card can be used in a faster slot.

PENTIUM 4 Intel's current mainstream processor.

PHENOM AMD's latest processor is designed for Socket AM2+ and AM3 motherboards, but can work with some older Socket AM2 boards, too.

PHONO
Hi-fi style interconnect, correctly known as an RCA jack and used for various audio and video connections. Red and white plugs are used for right and left audio channels, yellow for composite video.

POST Power-on self-test, performed by PCs when switched on, generating the text output that you see before Windows loads. Error messages are often displayed here, too.

PRIMARY CHANNEL
Most motherboards provide at least two IDE connectors for hard disks and other drives. The PC will boot from the master disk on the connector marked as the primary channel. The secondary channel is typically used for CD and DVD drives.

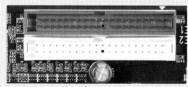

PS/2 CONNECTOR Used for keyboards and mice, although these now often connect via USB.

PSU Power supply unit. Refers to the device inside a PC that converts mains electricity and distributes it to the system's components, and also to the external mains adaptors supplied with some peripherals.

RAID Redundant array of inexpensive disks: a way of storing data on several hard disks to improve performance, or to provide a backup if one disk fails, or both. Modern motherboards support RAID on their PATA or SATA ports.

RAMBUS The company responsible for the expensive RDRAM type of memory used for a few years in Pentium III and Pentium 4 systems. Now obsolete and difficult to replace.

RCA See Phono.

RF Radio frequency, referring to the coaxial cable connection of TV antennas. An RF signal carries many video channels, while S-video and composite carry only one.

RIMM See Rambus.

RJ45 Plug used for Ethernet network cables, with eight wires. Larger than, but often mistaken for, RJ11.

SATA The Serial ATA interface is used for modern hard disks because it's faster and neater than PATA (Parallel ATA). The original SATA ran at 150MB/s, but the current standard has a 300MB/s mode, compared to PATA's maximum of 133MB/s.

SDRAM The memory type used by most Pentium II and Pentium III PCs. Common speeds are PC100 (100MHz) and PC133 (133MHz). Now obsolete.

SECONDARY CHANNEL See Primary Channel.

SERIAL PORT Old, slow port rarely used today but still present on many motherboards as a nine-pin connector.

SLAVE See Master.

SLI Nvidia's system for combining the power of two GeForce graphics cards in one PC. Also see CrossFire.

SOCKET 478 Intel's previous-generation processor socket, still supported by a handful of new motherboards and Pentium 4 and Celeron processors.

SOCKET M Socket for Intel's original mobile Core and Core 2 Duo Mobile processors. It has since been replaced with the newer Socket P.

SOCKET P Socket used by Intel's latest Core 2 mobile processors. It has the same number of pins as Socket M, but isn't backwards-compatible.

SOCKET 939 Socket used by AMD's Athlon 64 processors, including dual-core X2 versions. Supports processors with a dual memory controller.

SOCKET AM2 AMD's processor socket, which supports DDR2. Used by Athlon 64, Athlon FX and Sempron processors. Very similar to Socket 939, with one extra pinhole.

SOCKET AM2+ A newer AMD processor socket, which supports PC-8500 DDR2 memory and the Phenom range of processors. Backwards-compatible with older processors.

SOCKET AM3 AMD's latest processor socket, which supports DDR3 memory and the latest Phenom processors. This socket is not backwards-compatible with older AM2 or AM2+ processors.

S-VIDEO An average-quality analogue video connection with a four-pin cable.

TV-OUT Generic analogue output used for connection to a TV. Includes S-video and composite.

USB Universal serial bus. These ports are used to connect all manner of external devices.

USB2 The latest version of USB, which supports the Hi-Speed 480Mbit/s mode as well as older USB 1.1 devices.

VIVO Video in, video out. A compound connector on graphics cards that combines video inputs and outputs. Usually has a breakout cable that maps the pins to standard S-video or composite video connectors.

WEP Wired equivalent privacy. An encryption standard used to secure wireless networks. Comes in various strengths up to 256 bit, all weaker than WPA (below).

WIFI Name used collectively for the IEEE 802.11 wireless networking standards, including the 11Mbit/s 802.11b and 54Mbit/s 802.11g standards.

WPA WiFi protected access. An encryption standard used to secure wireless networks more reliably than WEP.

ZIF Zero insertion force: a processor socket where the chip is clamped using a lever.

THE COMPLETE PC REPAIR MANUAL

EDITORIAL
Editor
David Ludlow
david_ludlow@dennis.co.uk
Deputy Editor
Jim Martin
Production
Steve Haines
Design and layout
Anand Parmar

PHOTOGRAPHY
Danny Bird, Timo Hebditch, Andrew Ridge, Hugh Threlfall

ADVERTISING
Julie Price
ads.shopper@dennis.co.uk

INTERNATIONAL LICENSING
The content in this bookazine is available for international licensing overseas.
Contact Winnie Liesenfeld
+44 20 7907 6134, winnie_liesenfeld@dennis.co.uk

MANAGEMENT
Bookazine Manager
Dharmesh Mistry (020 7907 6100, dharmesh_mistry@dennis.co.uk)
Publishing Director
John Garewal
Operations Director
Robin Ryan
Group Advertising Director
Julian Lloyd-Evans
Circulation Director
Martin Belson

Finance Director
Brett Reynolds
Group Finance Director
Ian Leggett
Chief Executive
James Tye
Chairman
Felix Dennis

A DENNIS PUBLICATION
Dennis Publishing, 30 Cleveland St, London W1T 4JD. Company registered in England. All material © Dennis Publishing Limited, licensed by Felden 2009, and may not be reproduced in whole or part without the consent of the publishers.

Printed by Wyndeham Heron.

Dennis Publishing operates an efficient commercial reprints service. For more details, please call 020 7907 6640.

LIABILITY
While every care was taken during the production of this bookazine, the publishers cannot be held responsible for the accuracy of the information or any consequence arising from it. Dennis Publishing takes no responsibility for the companies featured in this bookazine.

The paper used within this bookazine is produced from sustainable fibre, manufactured by mills with a valid chain of custody.

ISBN 1-906372-89-6